FROM
BEHIND
—— THE ——
RED LINE

FROM
BEHIND
— THE —
RED LINE

An American Hockey Player In Russia

Tod Hartje with Lawrence Martin

MACMILLAN PUBLISHING COMPANY
NEW YORK

MAXWELL MACMILLAN CANADA
TORONTO

MAXWELL MACMILLAN INTERNATIONAL
NEW YORK   OXFORD   SINGAPORE   SYDNEY

Macmillan Publishing Company   Maxwell Macmillan Canada, Inc.
866 Third Avenue   1200 Eglinton Avenue East
New York, NY 10022   Suite 200
Don Mills, Ontario M3C 3N1

Macmillan Publishing Company is part of the Maxwell
Communication Group of Companies.

Library of Congress Cataloging-in-Publication Data
Hartje, Tod
From behind the red line: an American hockey
player in Russia/ by Tod Hartje with Law-
rence Martin.
p.   cm.
Includes index.
ISBN 0-02-548501-6
1. Hartje, Tod.   2. Hockey players—United States
—Biography.   3. Hockey—Soviet   Union.   I. Mar-
tin, Lawrence.   II. Title.
GV848.5.H37A3   1992   91-45139   CIP
796.962'092—dc20
[B]

Designed by Stephanie Bart-Horvath

Macmillan books are available at special discounts for
bulk purchases for sales promotions, premiums, fund-
raising, or educational use. For details, contact:

Special Sales Director
Macmillan Publishing Company
866 Third Avenue
New York, NY 10022

10   9   8   7   6   5   4   3   2   1

For Nicole; without her I would not be
where I am today. 143-7!

ACKNOWLEDGMENTS

When I first decided to spend a year playing and living in the Soviet Union, I had no idea what to expect. Fortunately, a host of people played instrumental roles both prior to and during my stay, helping me to remain upbeat and to see the positive aspects of the experience rather than the negative. I am deeply indebted to them for all they've done. Without them, this book would not have been possible.

First and foremost, my deepest thanks to everyone connected with the Sokol Kiev Hockey Club.

Next, I would like to thank the general manager of the Winnipeg Jets, Mike Smith, who was not only the architect of the exchange but was also responsible for giving me the initial impetus to write this book.

Special thanks to Lawrence Martin for taking me under his wing and turning this project into a polished work. It was a pleasure to deal with such an enthusiastic, efficient, amiable, and talented author. I appreciate the golf tips, too.

Thanks also to my editor, Rick Wolff, for believing in me and my progress despite the nearly impossible line of communication we were forced to maintain.

Many thanks as well to Lois Smith and Mara Buxbaum of PMK for their efforts in promoting and guiding me through the business end of this endeavor.

I will always remember the supportive letters and the strength I drew from all my friends: Lee Zeidman of CBS Sports; Dennis McDonald, Pat McDonald, Paul Henry, and Craig "Zinger" Heisinger of the Winnipeg

Jets; my agent, Bob Murray, and his secretary, Sue Brown; my nephews, Timothy and Tyler Mauthey; my niece, Jayme Hartje; my grandparents, Celia Hartje and Ralph and Helen Tresler; my uncle Al, aunt Mary, and cousins Tanya and Michelle Russell; my sister-in-law-to-be Melinda Peek; my brother-in-law, Todd Mauthey; my future in-laws Peter, Anita, Tom, and Kathy Sipos; Bill Cleary, Jr., and Ronn Tommasoni, my Harvard coaches; my closest friends, Jon Engels, Dave Boitz, Rick Wesp, and Dave Modec; Scott Beck; Jason Wengelin; Mark Maumer; Kate Roosevelt; Michelle Gustafson; Julie and Tina Clifford; Kim Cooper; Murry Gunty; Jennifer Samsel; Tim Perry; Mark Bianchi; Jenny Meyer; Becky Maukus; Cindi Ersek; Kate Felsen; Sandra Courdet; Todd and Jonelle Johnson; Jon and Jeaneen Mauthey; Andy Janfaza; Barb Berlin; Professor Ellsworth Feusch; Stacey Ostendorf; Ed and Sharon Engels; Dennis, Marlene, and Greyson Colvin; Ira and Rosemary Silver; Jimmy Devellano; my high school football coach, DeWayne Johnson, and his Sharon; my high school hockey coaches, Jack Peterson and Dave Notaro, Dave's wife, Joan, and daughters, Deanna and Kari; my ex-roommates, Jordan Schlachter, Bruce Miller, Brian Popiel, Chris Francazio, C. J. Young, Lane McDonald, Amy Rabow, and Julie Herlihy; my Harvard teammates, including John Murphy, Scott Farden, Allain Roy, and Kevin Sneddon.

Lastly, to my fiancée, Nicole Rival, my parents, Dale and Rochelle, my brothers, Jay and Tim, my sister, Tami Jo, and my future family, Dr. Jan, Eva, and Anita Rival—thanks!

—Tod Hartje

FOREWORD

An American playing professional hockey in the Soviet Union. It is an idea that has intrigued me since I first visited that country in 1975. I was in Moscow to attend a hockey coaches' symposium. I had also recently completed my doctorate in Russian studies and political science, which enabled me to look at the opportunity differently than most of the other coaches. I asked the Soviet hockey officials if I could coach in their country. They were open to my request, but I would need to be sponsored by the American Amateur Hockey Association. The Association told me they did not see what they would get out of it and denied my request for their sponsorship. But the idea of an American coaching or playing in the Soviet Union stayed with me. I also knew the Soviet hockey people would always be receptive toward it.

The participation of European hockey players in the National Hockey League has grown during the last fifteen years to the point that it is almost commonplace. A number of Swedes and Finns and a few Czechs have achieved star status. However, until recently, no Soviet players had played in the NHL. It was during the 1989–90 season that the first Soviet players were allowed to leave the USSR to play in North America. The players, Igor Larionov and Vladimir Krutov of Vancouver, Sergei Priakin and Sergei Makarov of Calgary, and Viacheslav Fetisov and Alexei Kasatonov of New Jersey were, for the most part, Soviet stars who were past their prime. However, it did appear that Soviet officials were now going to let their players go to the West. The NHL clubs increased their scouting and recruiting of Soviet players to coincide with this dramatic Soviet policy shift.

Why would the Winnipeg Jets send a player to the Soviet Union when the NHL clubs wanted players to move in the opposite direction? My academic background and experience has taught me that the Russians respect people who are willing to give them something, not just take from them. Their experience with the NHL made them believe the NHL wanted their players but did not give much of substance in return. The Winnipeg Jets want to get Soviet players and we will get them. More importantly, we want to have a relationship with the Soviets based on trust and respect, not on stealing their players. We would like them to tell us who they believe will be successful in the NHL and help us to develop them.

The Winnipeg Jets had set up an exchange agreement with Sokol Kiev, a team in the Ukrainian Republic city of Kiev, in 1988. It was the first formal agreement between a Soviet sports club and a North American professional sports team. The Jets and Sokol Kiev have had coaches and managers visit and work with each other. I believed it was time for us to send a player. Who would this player be, and would he go? I had someone in mind. He would have to be strong, bright, adventuresome, trusting, confident but a little naïve, plus be good enough to play in the Soviet Elite League. I also knew that this player would receive an incredible opportunity and experience.

Tod Hartje became this person. He had a lot going

for himself. He was from middle America—Anoka, Minnesota—had gone off to Harvard University to be educated, became a good college player with some potential to be a pro, and showed every indication he would be successful in life. Tod was not a bona fide NHL prospect. He needed to improve his overall ability to make it in the pros. I thought that the Soviet Union would be a good place for him to improve. Tod would also be unique if he agreed to go there. He would become the only person who would ever be able to say he was the first North American to play in Russia. It was now time to tell Tod.

Telling Tod turned out not to be difficult. I met with him in Boston on March 15, 1990. I ran through what I had in mind. He would play for Sokol Kiev and we would sign him to a contract. He would be paid rubles by Sokol Kiev and Canadian dollars by the Jets. It was simple. It would be a great opportunity, something that would always be beneficial to him. He was lucky, he would be the first foreign player to play in the Elite League.

Tod took this request as well as any stunned person would. He managed to ask a few questions. Will they take me? Yes, I have already spoken to them, they are quite enthusiastic about it. Where will I live? In the training center with the other players; it will be like living in a college dorm, no problem. The food? There is lots of food in the Ukraine, you will eat well, although the sameness of the meals will get to you, no problem. The language? The coach, Anatole Bogdanov, speaks some English, they will have a translator, and you will learn some Russian, no problem. Will I play? There is no guarantee; you will have to make the team and we think you will, but this could be a problem. Will I be accepted? Russians and Ukrainians are great people, you will be treated extremely well, no problem.

There were a few questions that Tod did not ask that he should have. Will the coach let me know how I am doing? Russian head coaches coach through intimidation, a reflection of their society, and rarely talk directly to the players. Will I be able to spend a lot of time on my own? Forget this too. You will be a Soviet athlete, your friends will be your teammates. Being a professional hockey player is hard work, real hard work, especially in Russia. Will I be able to keep in touch with my family, fiancée, and friends? Not likely. The training center has one phone, mail between countries takes four to six weeks. Look at it this way, you will have more time to work on your Russian, so do not worry about speaking English with people at home. Will the Jets keep in touch with me? Forget this, too. We believe people need to be strong. We will set it up, but you are on your own. Good luck.

Tod took a couple of weeks to think it over. We flew him to Winnipeg to meet the coach, Anatole Bogdanov. His Harvard teammates told him he was crazy if he went. But his parents and his fiancé told him to go, that it was too good to pass up. Tod also realized what a great opportunity and life experience it would be once he got over the shock. He acknowledged that, like most people, he would like to be unique, and playing hockey in Russia certainly was not a routine accomplishment. I think he liked it when I said, "You will get to visit and play in Gorki and would likely be the first American who was not a CIA spy in that city in twenty years." For whatever reason people decide to do different, maybe crazy, things, he agreed to go.

I knew what we were asking Tod to do was tough, real tough. But I also knew that Tod was a strong individual, tough enough to survive, smart enough to adapt, and that he would grow as a player and a person and be successful. I knew that, in the beginning, Tod would be humbled by the country but would, in time, become almost Russian. This experience was to enable Tod to do something many of us have always wanted to do but could not—to live in the Soviet Union as a Soviet citizen. He would live and travel as a Soviet athlete, and he would come to see the country and the people through the Russian eyes of an American.

There would be some notoriety back home in America but very little notoriety or special treatment in Russia. Tod's life as a Soviet elite athlete would not be as hard as the lives of the Russian people, but, it would be a lot harder than the lives his Harvard classmates would be facing. How hard? Tod would show up in the middle of Russia around July 1 unable to speak Russian. His physical conditioning would be substantially lower than his teammates'. He would quickly become impatient, almost agitated, with what would seem to be a ponderously slow and backward way of life.

Tod would learn to endure and survive. He would have to. All Russians learn to endure and survive.

—Michael A. Smith
General Manager
Winnipeg Jets

1

Growing up, not far from Minneapolis in the two-bar town of Anoka, all that mattered to me and every other kid was the game. Street football, pickup basketball, ice hockey. Name it, we played it. The neighborhood was filled with children, future stars all of us, and we had the best deal imaginable—sports every day.

As long as my grades were good, my parents, both teachers, encouraged the sporting life. Mom was a beauty queen in college and a fine athlete herself. Dad was once a star football lineman. My appetite for sport was bred in the bone and there wasn't one sport I didn't want to dominate. I boxed, wrestled, golfed. I threw the football a mile and in one hockey game that we won by a score of 7–1, I got terrifically lucky and scored six goals.

Anoka was the best. Every corner you turned, excited faces on rushing bodies. Nothing else to think about— least of all the Russians.

The Russians in my early years existed only as a hostile stereotype of the subconscious. Mom and Dad had taught me to be open-minded, free of prejudice, but that was kind of impossible in a country where one's friends knocked the Russians all the time and where Ronald Reagan, a president I respected, spoke of the evil empire to the east. Even with the advent of Mikhail Gorbachev and his glasnost freedoms, it was hard for me not to buy into the prevailing image of the Russians as a force of darkness. Of course at that time, I didn't know, never imagined, that before too long I'd be joining them, joining them for that last year their communist system existed.

From high school in Anoka I'd gone on, in 1986, to a college that was not the one of my choice—Harvard. The preppy, private school syndrome never appealed to me. I was more inclined toward a place where the sporting calendar offered more—the University of Denver. My parents' reasoning prevailed however and I was off, with my 3.9 grade point average, to the pick of the Ivy League. There, my folks and others had determined, my oversized ego would get its deflationary due.

Being an athlete, an instant member of the Harvard hockey team, I wound up in the jock dorm. While the so-called intellects ruminated at Adams House, we sweaty types kicked beer cans at Kirkland. On my floor, where a big sign read "Wake Me for Reading Period," there was ample space behind the couch, and upon finishing a can of Busch, the idea was to put a nice sputnik-arc jumpshot into said landing area. When the pile grew so high it was coming back over the top of the couch at us, we'd gather up the empties and cash in the aluminum. One time our beer can mountain fetched us more than a hundred dollars, enough to get us off to a big start on the next heap.

It was at Harvard that I got my first look at a real live Russian. At the hockey rink one day, I was moving stuff around with our equipment manager, the laugh-a-minute, swear-king Chet Stone. In town was a hockey team called Sokol Kiev. As part of an exhibition swing, they were to play us the next night and we were planning on knocking their jaws off.

As Chety and I did our work, the Sokol (as in "local") players came by to drop off their equipment. Instantly, the stereotype was confirmed for me. In their fur hats these guys looked blank, sour, implacably hostile. Chety, no Russian-lover he, caught wind of the odor coming from their equipment and almost gagged. I hadn't smelled anything so bad in years. When they left, Stone began kicking their bags all over the room. I joined in, then we ran for clean air.

Injured for the first time in my Harvard career, I couldn't play in the game against the Soviets and was really annoyed about it. The Russians were among the most talented players in the world. These were players who you wanted to test yourself against. Technical wizards on the ice, their elite squads had beaten the best from the NHL, from Canada, from the United States. They played a swifter, cleaner, purer game, hockey ballet-style.

But having heard the flattering notices I still wasn't prepared for the mastery of the game the team from Kiev showed that night. The shifts, the weaving, the changing of gears, the light feet, the ticktacktoe passing

3

precision. Compared to the alley-fight style of North American hockey, this was a different game. It was art. These guys belonged in Adams House.

On their American tour they were victorious in every other match, but by some strange bit of happenstance we tied them. The score was 4–4, though a more just verdict, given their clear superiority in controlling the play, would have been 14–4. Shot after shot rang off our goalposts, and when their blasts were on target, our goalie's glove would appear like the hand of God. To most of our players, it was only right that God would help us out. We were, after all, morally superior.

The next day, with our skaters still bitching about how they almost retched every time they skated in the corner with the "commie bastards," the Russians were gone and I soon forgot about them.

I was in my senior year of a history major then and planning to try out for the Winnipeg Jets of the NHL following graduation. In Minnesota I had been an all-state first-team all-star on graduation from high school and had been expecting to get drafted then. But I was happy when the Jets selected me after my freshman year at Harvard.

Through college I never heard from Winnipeg except for the odd Christmas card and so I was surprised shortly after the Kiev team left town when Jets general manager Mike Smith rang me up. In Boston to see his club play the Bruins, Smith invited me to his hotel suite. He didn't say much at first, so I inquired about the team's plans for me. "We rate players on the basis of three categories," Smith said. "The first is the sure-bet NHLers, the second is the maybe gang, and the third is for those who have no chance of making the big leagues. You are in the middle group."

My college career hadn't been outstanding so this didn't surprise me. Smith then started talking about international hockey. His team had a history of developing players from Europe and of sending North Americans over there for training. As it was clear he was angling toward something, my thoughts began to brighten. The prospect of a year or two in Europe—Sweden, Switzerland, France—was a tantalizing notion.

Then, in his laconic manner, Smith looked over at me and dropped the bombshell: "In your case Tod, we'd like to send you to the Soviet Union to play for a season there."

As my jaw dropped he went on. "We feel it would be good for your development, both from the point of view of gaining experience as a person and as a hockey player.

"In life the people who are successful are the ones who go the extra mile. You'll learn the Soviet hockey system, their skills. You'll learn the language, the culture."

Though it seemed clear the Winnipeg GM wasn't kidding, I asked, "Are you kidding?" His look said no. He wanted me to go suit up for the enemy.

Not your typical NHL executive, Smith was the holder of a doctorate in Soviet studies. He knew the Soviet game, wanted to get the lead on Western hockey ties with the Russians, and with Gorbachev's openness the opportunity was ripe to do this—to break the Soviet barrier. No North American had ever played on a Soviet pro hockey team. Smith wanted me to be the first.

Smith liked the idea of sending someone with a Harvard background. The Soviets had heard of Harvard and the GM thought a Harvard man would be looked upon with more respect by the Soviets than some toothless goon with a grade-four education. He also thought my playing style would be suited to the Soviet way. I was a passer, more than a shooter, and the Soviets were famous for their passing game.

Quietly reeling, I asked Smith what Soviet team he wanted to send me to. "In the Ukraine, there's a team called Sokol," he said. "Sokol Kiev."

I thought of the locker-room scene, the alien looks, the Chet Stone descriptives, but most of all I thought of the talent I had seen on the Kiev team. They were so good. How could I make it with them? They'd skate sickles around me.

Smith now pulled out five or six books on the USSR he thought I should read and suggested I might take a Berlitz course in the language. "Naturally you'll want to take a while to think about this."

It was late March. Final exams were in April, graduation in June, and I was to be in Kiev for the start of their training camp by the first of July.

Kiev was fifty miles from Chernobyl. Governments were still keeping diplomats out of Kiev for fear of radiation hits. I knew not a word of Russian or Ukrainian. I'd heard more about the KGB than the Soviet hockey league. But I'd read that Soviet teams trained year-round, isolated in barracks, shut off from wives, family, a normal life. Igor Larionov, the star who escaped to the NHL, compared the atmosphere to a concentration camp. Slava Fetisov, the remarkable defenseman who also fled the iron-fisted hockey dictatorship of Viktor

6

Tikhonov, said the system turned players into "ice robots."

How could I live with them? How could I skate with them? How could I communicate with them? How could I stand their food, or their lack of food? The newspaper reports said their society was falling apart. I knew that some Westerners lived over there as media correspondents, diplomats, businessmen. But they had their own setups, their own little Western infrastructures. They weren't employed as a cog deep inside a closed Soviet organization like I would be. And they weren't twenty-two years old.

From Boston I phoned my parents. "Dad, they want me to go play in the Soviet Union." I phoned my girlfriend, Nicole Riva. She was Czech. Her parents had fled Czechoslovakia, her mother stuffed in the trunk of a car, in 1968, the year the Soviets staged an armed invasion to smash a democratic uprising. "Nikki, they want me to go play in the Soviet Union."

We all pawed around the idea for some time, but in the end the word from each party was the same. "Tod, you can't pass up an opportunity like this." Opposition came from Harvard teammates and other friends. Their advice: The system's rotten, the food's rotten, the KGB will run your life. Don't do it. Though I was leaning more to my parents' and Nicole's counsel and that of other senior people who were more positive, I was mindful of one thing—those teammates I'd talked to had been there. Eyewitnesses.

Smith invited me to Winnipeg because, as chance would have it, the coach of the Sokol team, Anatole Bogdanov, was visiting. I was encouraged when I saw him. With a big smile, big white teeth, fashionable clothes, personable air, and good facility in the English language, he appeared refreshingly un-Russian.

Soviet players were excited at the prospect of my coming, he told me. "Good for relations between our countries. We will make you comfortable." But though I was around Bogdanov a fair bit, I went away with very little information. Nothing about how he would use me on the team, about how their schedule worked, about political troubles in the Soviet Union. No curiosity about me. No questions from him on my background, my family, my hockey skills, my style of play.

He did ask one thing. "Do you want any special treatment?" I could picture his mind working—"Our Russian system is tougher. Better offer this wimp a softer training regimen."

"No," I said quickly. "I want to be treated just like the others."

In a Winnipeg newspaper interview, Bogdanov spoke mainly in generalities, but did invoke the Harvard connection. "Hartje went to Harvard, so I know he has brains." I should have told him that the two don't necessarily go hand in hand.

Back in Boston I ran a little every day while studying for exams but had no time for any special physical training or to study the Russian language. The whole idea of me on a Soviet hockey team seemed too farfetched. My mind couldn't fix on it. I was too American.

Thoughts focused more on my girlfriend Nicole and what the Soviet exile would do to our relationship. She had become the big part of my life, so much so that engagement was in the air. Unbelievable as it seemed to my buddies in Kirkland House, I was changing from the small-town kid who arrived at the big college with arrogance in abundance. At first, Harvard was adolescence extended. Life in the brain lane still meant all the sports, beer, and girls I could handle.

Nicole had taken strong exception to this attitude. She was turned off the first day she met me at the dorm. I had my shirt off, as I often did, and she thought this was supervain. She continued her loathing for some time, riled that other girls appeared such pushovers that they even stooped to help me with my laundry. In that, my freshman year, I went so long without cleaning my clothes that the stacks of dirty socks and shirts reached almost as high as the beer cans. I'd brought about forty pair of socks and boxers, and an equal number of shirts though, so I wondered—what's the big deal?

Somehow Nicole came to find me less and less obnoxious. We got along well at the parties where I wore a shirt and we became nondating friends. By third year, having pretty well explored the field, I decided to turn the friendship into something more than that and soon we were together all the time. She knew as much about hockey as any guy did. More importantly, she was less parochial, more career-oriented and able to speed up my maturing process, getting me out of the toy department into the real world.

She was apprehensive, understandably so given my reputation, and she naturally wondered how I could possibly stay faithful when in Russia for so long. I pulled out some pictures of incredibly dumpy Russian women driving tractors to ease her concern. In truth though, I had probably become more dependent on Nicole than her on me, and I suppose this was demonstrated by my presenting her with an engagement ring before I left.

On June 7, I graduated, then tried to get in a couple of weeks' holiday before departure date. Time didn't permit a reading of the books Smith had given me or any study of the Russian language. The result was that I departed for the Soviet Union knowing all of four words in Russian—da, nyet, spasiba, and babushka. Translation—yes, no, thank you, and grandma.

Working on the combinations I could even come up with a sentence: "No thank you grandma!"

As I boarded the plane for the evil empire, I couldn't help thinking that this was the answer I should have given when this whole idea was broached in the first place. "No thank you grandma."

2

My dad's final words of advice: "Maintain a positive attitude, son, and it will all work out."

At the airport in New York, groups were setting off on excursion packages to Moscow and Leningrad. Their holidaying enthusiasm contrasted my deep skepticism. They were going for three weeks; I was going for an eternity.

On board I began reading *The Hunt for Red October* but was distracted by the rattling of bottles in the back, in the smoking section. Poking my head through the curtain I could barely see for the cigarette fumes, but noticed many Russian passengers already well into the sauce. Airplane mini–booze bottles adorned their trays like marching bands. Throughout the flight they consumed their national drink, vodka, in magnificent quantity. By the time we reached our destination, they were comfortably comatose.

"They work, they drink, they sleep," someone had said, summing up the treadmill existence of the average Russian. The drinking extended to the workplace—in my case the hockey arena. A Canadian living in Moscow once played on a factory-league team on which, he recalled, his linemates took shots of vodka between shifts. In one game he noticed a teammate was abstaining and playing exceptionally well. "See what a little clean living can do?" the Canadian said enthusiastically. The Russian, with an air of condescension, looked at him. "I had a half a bottle before I came to the rink," he said.

At the Moscow airport a grim-looking customs official fired questions at me like I was up on a murder rap. When he found out I was in the Winnipeg Jets organization, the mood changed. Now he was friendly and angling for a souvenir. Remembering that millions of young Russians collected pins, I gave him one from the Jets and was on my way.

In the poorly lit lobby, I stood for about twenty minutes until a tall pale man stepped forward introducing himself as Anatole Khromov, a government official representing the Kiev team. On the way into Moscow, where we would overnight before flying on to Kiev, I was struck by the number of broken-down automobiles, about one every block. Everything was so rundown, so old, I thought I was moving back decades in time. Cars were lined up forever at the gas stations, their drivers standing beside them smoking, chatting, reading papers. Along the immensely wide roads, drivers changed lanes with random blindness, causing a goodly number of collisions, this perhaps explaining the many crippled vehicles by curbside. At the stop-lights, motorists would line up about ten abreast, rev-ving their wheezing machines, creating so much din it reminded me of the Indy starting line. All that was missing was a grand marshal to shout, "Gentlemen, start your coffins!"

Having made it to the hotel safely, we sat down to din-ner in a hotel reserved for Communist party officials of the Ukraine. There were just the two of us, but in a mo-ment our table was filled with enough booze, great flasks of vodka and cognac, to submerge a party of twelve. Khromov, in the Soviet way, began the toasts. We toasted the motherland, we toasted friendship, we toasted the soil, the United States. We toasted mothers, fathers, grandchildren. We toasted hockey. Khromov was no dif-ferent from the Soviets I'd seen on the plane. Half-cut be-fore our food even arrived and therefore unable (fortunately) to assess the quality, I was already wonder-ing whether I'd be able to survive the year, liver intact.

At the airport the next morning hundreds pushed like refugees toward a single ticket booth. Being with Khromov, I didn't have to queue up with the plebs. But not by accident we ended up standing right next to the hard-currency shop, one of the many such stores that are off-limits to ruble-carrying Russians. Khro-mov shuffled around the window display, finally fixing his protruding forehead on the cartons of foreign cig-arettes.

"Marlboros!" he proclaimed. "My favorite cigarette, Marlboros!" He was puffing on some stale-smelling Rus-sian thing. "Our cigarettes no good. American better."

He went on in this unsubtle vein for some time until I determined there really wasn't much choice but to take the flagrant hint. I went in and bought him a carton of Marlboros with my American dollars.

On the flight to Kiev, Khromov told me I would get a lot out of this Soviet venture if I kept my eyes and ears open. (Yes, I felt like replying, just the way I did at the foreign currency store.) He was going on and on, and I was annoyed at the airport gambit and wanted to tell him to shut up so I could sleep.

But I veered to attention when, as a sly smile crossed his face, Khromov let a big one slip out. "By the way, Tod," he said quietly. "We have arranged pretty Russian girl for you."

I stammered for a minute, not knowing what to say. Khromov, who like many Russians leaves out the articles when he speaks English, added: "This is best way to learn Russian language. Sleep with girl."

"Jeezus," I told myself. "I haven't even arrived yet and they've already lined up the spy." I explained that I had a girlfriend back home and we were engaged to get married. Khromov was not discouraged. "Aw, dis no problem, dis no problem. America, thousands of miles away. You will like Russian girl."

In addition to teaching me the language, the appointed lady would be my personal guide, he explained, taking me on tours of the city, making sure I got everything I needed. Green, just out of college, naturally suspicious, I wanted someone who had experience in dealing with the Soviets to talk to about this. I didn't know how to react. I didn't want to give an outright "no thank you." In my situation I would no doubt be in need of some kind of guide for help on any number of things. But at the same time I couldn't help wondering what this Russian girl would look like. Nicole had mentioned how I was maturing, cleaning up my act in respect to other women. Maybe this would be the test.

I signaled neutrality in my response to Khromov, showing neither favor nor disfavor with the idea. This was 1990. The spy stuff was getting a little old hat by now with the breaking down of the cold war and all the new thinking that was going on. But I knew the KGB was still the mammoth police-state structure it had always been, and I couldn't be sure I wouldn't be used.

It was almost dark when we arrived in Kiev but my first look at the city was invigorating. It was handsome, full of glorious architecture, flowers, soft green foliage, wide, clean boulevards, smartly dressed pedestrians—an overall brightness I hadn't imagined possible in the Soviet Union.

Before going to the Sokol Kiev training base where I would reside, Khromov took me to another liquid dinner at the Hotel Soyuz. Our booze bill here made the previous one look modest. The taste buds were suitably killed off before the main fare arrived and it became, like the first one, another no-memory meal. I was a willing recipient of the drinks but already starting to ask myself questions. Shouldn't I be more careful? Wasn't this pouring on of the drinks by design? The theory, as many of my sexist college buddies would attest after one-night stands, was as old as could be—the inebriated eye is much more forgiving than the sober one. Stay clear-headed Tod, I told myself, so you can judge what the hell is going on around here.

At the training base, my first thought was to phone Nicole and tell her, not about the designated Helga, but just that I had made it here. After a fruitless search in my room I found a phone in the lobby. But all I could get was a loud beeping noise. I didn't understand that you don't just pick up a phone in this country and dial long distance. So with my tiny Russian dictionary I started looking up the word for operator. The attendant on duty approached, but he didn't speak a word of English, and when I pointed at the Detroit phone number I'd written down he looked at me strangely. In rapid-fire Russian he began lecturing me. His voice got louder and louder and he got closer and closer till I could smell his walnut breath. I'm thinking, "clue in, dope! Isn't it obvious I don't speak a word of your language?" But while I tried to politely pantomime what I wanted to do, he kept at me until I was almost ready to slug him. In a rage I went upstairs and crashed.

The next morning players were beginning to arrive in camp. It was the first of July, the beginning of their eleven-month hockey season. While the NHLers would be walking the golf courses and riding the beach surf until mid-September, Soviet hockey players had finished their one-month annual respite and now got set to train in the sun.

The first people I met were two men wearing big white aprons with food splattered all over them. Brilliantly deducting that they were the cooks, I introduced myself, and for lack of better communication possibilities, we quickly entered into a game of charades. Other employees of the base, or baza, came by, made an effort to be nice, but all I could do was stand there like a nodding, smiling illiterate, repeating one of the words in my four-word Russian vocabulary. *Spasiba, spasiba, spasiba.* The more I did so, the more I thought about how we used to mock Asian and Mexican immigrants to the United States who could only repeat ad nauseam a couple of words of English. Now I knew how they felt.

Soon the cooks were back and one of them was throwing an imaginary ball into the air, then swinging an imaginary racket at it. Wimbledon! I thought. Wimbledon was on TV and they wanted me to go and watch it with them. Soon, however, we arrived at a Ping-Pong table where they took turns trying to show me how the game was played. They were friendly matches, but they got annoyed at me for my style of serving. They threw the ball in the air before serving, much more difficult than my way of simply holding it in the hand and letting it drop.

"Nyet, nyet," they stammered as I continued doing this. "Da, da," I retorted. "Da, da."

It was my first all-Russian conversation. I congratulated myself on the repartee.

The baza was located about thirty-five miles from downtown Kiev. A four-story white plaster structure with spacious wood balconies and a gently inclining tan roof, the residence was enveloped by tall stands of forest and apparently radiation-free air. On the main floor were the kitchen, dining room, coach's quarters, offices, and every telephone in the place—two of them. The middle two floors housed all the players in reasonably spacious quarters, and the top level was the recreation zone. It contained the Ping-Pong room, a snooker table with no balls or cues, a big TV center with reclining chairs, and the most unused area in the place—the library.

In addition there was an adjacent smaller building with a weight room, a bicycle storage area, a dentist's chamber, and a handball court under construction. Outside were two worn-down tennis courts on which lay a couple of balls that looked like they hadn't been used since the Krushchev era.

The Sokol camp was said to be about the highest in quality of any in the Soviet hockey league. It was situated among other posh residences for Soviet clubs and organizations. Nearby was a children's hospital and a war vets' home for soldiers who got messed up in the head in Afghanistan.

I was soon to learn that the room they chose for me, this probably unbeknownst to management, was the most strategically located of any in the camp. I had two comfortably furnished rooms on a corner of the second floor with a large balcony fronting a scenic wooded area. The importance of this location lay in the fact that it afforded the only access to the building, excepting the main entrance. My balcony was reachable from the top of a fence that swung around the corner of the residence. One could scale the fence, stand on top of it, get up onto the porch, and enter my room. It wasn't easy, but for players who missed curfew, or who wanted to sneak a girl in, or who violated drinking regulations, Hartje corner was the only hope.

While checking out the baza facilities I was more than

mildly struck by another feature—there was no hockey rink. Tennis courts, weight rooms, acres upon acres of pleasant woods, but no hockey arena and no plan to build one. The nearest ice surface was thirty miles away. This meant piling into a bus every day, sometimes twice a day, for a forty-five minute drive there and back.

Kiev's population, two and a half million, ranked it third in the Soviet Union behind Moscow and Leningrad. But the city, a reasonably popular hockey locale, had only two covered ice rinks—this compared to dozens of such structures in hockey cities in North America. As well as the appalling state of supplies and equipment, this dismal lack of facilities was prevalent throughout the Soviet Union. Yet the Soviet Union had become a major world power, sometimes "the" major world power in the sport. Maybe this experiment would help me find out the answer to the question, how? What is it that makes Soviet athletes tick?

My first day I met some of the Sokol players and it was apparent, at least it seemed apparent, that none among them spoke decent English. At a team meeting in the evening, Coach Bogdanov introduced me and another new player to the team. I had no idea what the coach told them about me, and Bogdanov made no effort to translate his words.

I repaired to my room for a few minutes' study of the Cyrillic alphabet before heading to the dining room for my first meal with the whole team. I was seated with three of the youngest players and, unable to communicate, we exchanged half-embarrassed glances the whole meal. The coaches sat at a separate table and were served by a waitress. We got up and got our own.

19

Salad was the starter, and as I took my first bite, two words leapt to mind—Chernobyl vegetables. Before I lit into a contaminated carrot or a radiation radish, I wanted to ask the guys if the stuff was safe. But that was impossible. I don't know why Bogdanov sat me here without even introducing me. Seemed like no thought went into it.

The main course was chicken and, to my pleasant surprise, the meat was less tough than a hockey puck. In fact, my expectations were exceeded to the point I wanted more, and without thinking about it I got up and headed for the counter. As I did I noticed dead silence fell over the place. Looking over my shoulder I saw that everyone had stopped eating and was looking at me, freeze-framed, like in an E. F. Hutton commercial. I realized then that you don't get second helpings here and skulked back to the table feeling like an idiot. One plateful was the rule, and it was gulped down hurriedly. I was used to lingering at meals over the family table at home. Here it was gobble, gobble, gobble, and gone.

I tried a couple of unidentifiable-looking creatures at that first meal and they made me gag. One was a soggy oat ball that tasted like rancid porridge. Every time it appeared on my plate—and it did with almost every meal—I felt like picking it up and heaving it through the window. Actually, if I had pitched it up to the ceiling it probably would have stuck on it. Washing the oat balls down was difficult for me because you couldn't drink tap water and all they served was bottled stuff. Far from Evian, Soviet bottled water had an oily texture, and as it slid down your throat it felt like a garter snake. For milk they had a thick, sour cream potion called kafir. My first haul on it gave me the dry heaves. I tried mixing spoonfuls of sugar in it to lessen the sourness, but the anguish was only marginally eased.

Maintain a good attitude, I kept telling myself. I had been in the Soviet Union only a day and already I was missing Nicole, already I was anxious to talk to someone from back home, already I was lonely.

The next morning, we had a long-distance run scheduled, but before it the team captain, Valery Sherayev, waved me over to his car. He had a Volga, the upscale choice among the two staple automobiles in the Soviet Union, the other being the Zhiguli (Lada), a model of such thin-tin construction it looked bendable by hand.

Sherayev opened his trunk, pulled out a couple of soft drinks, signaled me into the car, popped a tape in the stereo, and we were off. It was a nice feeling, a little like cruising the city with one of my buddies. Remarkable on the central sidewalks were the number of old women, beefy babushkas who tunneled their way through anything in their path. The twenty million lost in World War II, mainly men, had left a gender gap that now extended to the senior set. There just weren't enough men to go around. But besides the babushkas, many younger ladies were in evidence, and in contrast to the dressed-down style of so many young American women, almost all the Kievites were in heels and dresses. It wasn't high-quality clothing, but they were making the best of what they had and they looked attractive in a sweet and feminine kind of way.

We drove around, stopped at the market where Sherayev bought me a bag of raspberries and made me feel
like a comrade. He knew a few English words, one of
them being "box." "Now we go to box," he said. "Now,
go to box."

Not knowing what he meant, I decided to be agree-
able and replied, "Yes, okay box." Sliding into the ver-
nacular, I quickly amended that to "Da, okay box."

While I tried to figure out what he had in mind, Sherayev drove several miles away from anything to get to
his box. We finally came upon it—it was a small garage
where he stored his car.

Soviets, I learned, don't have garages at their homes
or apartments, but are allotted garage space in random locations around the city. Sherayev could keep his
car at the training base, where there was space. But
when he lived in his apartment with his family he
could only keep it in his box, meaning about a half
hour's bus ride each day just to get his car. He and the
others seemed to accept this ludicrous setup as the
normal run of things.

On this day Sherayev entered his box and came back
with a can of gasoline to tank up. When getting gas,
Soviet motorists often purchase extra cans to cut down
on their number of times in one-hour lineups.

Back at the camp we did a 10K run, which was fine
but for the fact that I didn't know that it would be 10K
and therefore had no idea how to pace myself. The occasion afforded me my first glance at the obtuse idea of
sartorial splendor among Soviet athletes. With their
gym shorts and sneakers, many wore colored nylon

socks. Some went a step further and sported cheap argyles pulled halfway up the calf. During the run with them I felt like I was in nerd city.

Our first practice that evening was a scrimmage. I had played forward almost all my career, but with no explanation Bogdanov now put me on defense. I was in a totally strange environment to begin with. Why not make it more strange? Was this the same smiling, communicative Bogdanov I had met in Winnipeg?

He called me over to the center of the ice while the others were doing stretches and introduced me to my defensive partner. I couldn't make out his name; Bogdanov had to repeat it about seven times, and I still didn't know what he was talking about and was embarrassed to hell. It was Viacheslava—Viacheslava Timchenko. The common short form for this first name is the much simpler Slava. Why didn't the coach just introduce Viacheslava, who was looking at me like I was a real prick during all this, as Slava and leave it at that?

Slava and I couldn't talk to each other, but he would whack me on the shoulder on the bench when it was time for us to go on the ice. The scrimmage was fast, too fast. These guys hadn't been on the ice in over a month but looked like they were in midseason form. I was used to opening-day camps at Harvard where everyone lolled around. Here the skating, the passing, the scoring were crisp—on all the plays except the ones in which I was involved. The run in the morning, the changed time zones, the different food left me feeling shaky. After a couple of shifts I went to get the water bottle from the bench. I looked around. There was none. These guys didn't have water at practices, not even that bottled oily stuff.

They were all looking at me, of course, sizing up with grim faces the new Amerikanski, and all I wanted to do was hide. I wanted to run and hide and tell Dad that his advice wasn't working, tell him that good attitudes don't work on different planets.

3

First thing every morning, in dress shoes and polyester sweat suits, or some other elegant mix, the Russian and Ukrainian players with me among them would gather at the front entrance of the residence. There, like soldiers, we would form into a perfectly straight line and in turn shout out what number we stood in the row. It being established that none of us had vaporized in the night, then and only then could the day begin.

Had someone died or fled, it would have been apparent, count or no count. But the routine was in keeping with the authoritarian cut of the Soviet hockey system, indeed of Soviet society as a whole before the communist fall. In the minds and hopes of many it was a system on its last legs. But tradition was dying hard in Kiev. Though he did it with a smile, Bogdanov was running this hockey team in the draconian manner in which he was reared. No one dared question his judgment. No one dared question him on anything. The players would openly jest about problems on the team, but never about the coach. They cowered under him, afraid to take the initiative. Even when crises developed, say an illness in the family, they would be afraid to approach Bogdanov.

When I wrote Nicole that the coach had put me on defense, where I didn't want to be, she responded that I must talk to him about it. At home I was the type who liked to bring problems out in the open, always had been. At Harvard I had a coach, Bill Cleary, who was open and fun to play for. If I had something I wanted to discuss with him I didn't hesitate. He ran a class operation, always conscious of doing something that was not part of the mind-set here—stressing the positive.

We had a little rule on the Harvard team—you could never mention the word "lose." If the coach heard the word or an approximation of it, you were on the floor for fifty push-ups. If he slipped up and used it himself, he'd get down and do fifty. The need didn't arise often however, because we were usually winners. We reached the final four of the NCAA tournament my first year, and in my third, playing the finals in Minnesota, we won the national championship.

Our style was basically clean hockey, certainly clean by NHL standards. If you got into a scuffle you were to skate directly away from it. The intellectual atmosphere of the college was supposed to extend itself to the rink. Still, our hockey was nothing like the ballets the Russians put on. We had a defenseman from Canada, Kevin Melrose, who was the most hated guy in the league. Melrose had a punch that could knock down a wall. In a game against Brown University, he one-timed three of their players, left them lying on the ice like stiffs. Harvard fans, who didn't normally take to one player, went crazy over Melrose, even organizing a fan club. The big defenseman, who was talented with the puck and could skate, had this thing about Brown. In another game he kayoed their captain and cocaptain. He snapped the former's collarbone with one jolting check and broke the other's arm when he flattened him into the boards like a pop can. These things didn't happen in Soviet hockey.

Coach Cleary was the same Bill Cleary who starred for the U.S.A. in our gold-medal victory over the Russians at the Olympics in Squaw Valley in 1960. Before him in my senior year in high school I was coached in a tournament by Herb Brooks, the architect of our other hockey gold—the Lake Placid Olympics in 1980.

By coincidence, I seem fated for the Russian connection. I went from Brooks to Cleary to the guy who had the Ph.D. on the Soviets, Mike Smith, and finally to the Soviets themselves.

I had to be sensitive to the traditions of the Soviet game. I couldn't come in, rock the boat, try to start changing the way they did things. So I decided against taking Nicole's advice and, for the time being, kept my mouth shut.

Change was certainly on the way. In Moscow in the late '80s, the great players of the Soviet game had rebelled against the totalitarianism of Coach Tikhonov. Fetisov, sick of being browbeaten, had once stood up at the bench, grabbed Tikhonov by the lapels of his jacket and thrust him backward. As the startled hockey dictator struggled to regain his balance, Fetisov turned and walked away. The outburst was one of many glasnost-inspired challenges that gained Soviet players more freedom, including the right to play in foreign countries. But while Fetisov, Larionov, Sergei Makarov and others had the stature to stand up to the bosses and get away with it, players in Kiev and other provincial capitals still succumbed to the old command system.

At our camp, once you got past Bogdanov, things did lighten up some. The team's assistant coach was a squat man with a fat belly who had a tendency to blow off a lot of steam. The players called him Chinik. I thought this was a curious-sounding Russian name. Then somebody told me the word meant "teapot." The players were calling him Teapot. How fitting. He looked just like one.

Teapot, whose real name was Alexander Fadeyev, carried out all the Bogdanov's commands. He ran the routine practices and exercise sessions, he did room checks, he spied on the drinkers, the smokers, the fornicators. When the guys were up to no good, they usually had someone on Teapot patrol to spot him steaming down the hall. He had the coach's ear and therefore power, but it was hard to take Teapot seriously. He wore the same suit every day, its special feature being sleeves that came down to the fingertips. This gave him a man-without-hands look, but it didn't catch as a fashion trend, even among the Soviets. The quiet word around camp was that the only reason Teapot had the job was because he was a close personal friend of Bogdanov's. No one respected his hockey knowledge.

I had even less communication with him in the first few weeks than I did with the head coach. Teapot and I exchanged not a word, only suspicious glances. But I did have one friend at the top—the team's physician, a guy whose name I never did get straight and simply called the doc. Doc was a big strong man of about sixty who always wore a blue American college sweatshirt and who, like so many Soviet doctors, was a big nicotine fan, smoking a couple of packs of cigarettes a day. What mattered to me was that he spoke English. He carried a dictionary around at all times and, keen on learning more words even at his age, made a point of sitting beside me on the bus. There he would complain that his country was so absurd that "it pay bus driver as much as me."

The doc was negative on almost all aspects of Soviet society except its women. It wasn't long after getting to know me that, in the spirit of Mr. Khromov, he came forward with gratuitous advice. "You need Russian girl, Tod," he said. "Russian girl make you happy." It was early yet and I still hadn't been introduced to the girl Khromov had lined up for me. In the case of the doc though, the advice on ladies was coming from a real pro. He was known around the camp as a swordsman extraordinaire. Unmarried—"why bother when you have what I do"—he often had two or three women, many years his younger, in his room with him at the base.

Initially he was the only person there with whom I could have a real conversation. He would drop into my room with his language books and we'd teach each other—the only interruption being his frequent smoke breaks. "Wait, I must smoke," he would say every few minutes. "I must smoke." Knowing that I was an abstainer, he insisted on going outside onto my balcony to smoke, even in midwinter.

At the base, the doc didn't appear to do much doctoring. A trainer or a nurse did most of the routine stuff while Doc sort of hung out, dispensing advice to Teapot and Bogdanov on the condition of the players. He didn't have much equipment to work with. I noticed things were a little behind in the technology department my first day at the base when I saw workmen cutting the large lawn areas by hand, with scythes. The only lawn mowers in this country, I was told, were in use at the Kremlin.

The equipment in the medical room looked like leftovers from the siege of Leningrad. For testing my lungs and breathing capacity they strapped me on a rickety machine and jammed an old vacuum hose down my throat. The nurse used soap and water to lubricate a suction cup for checking my heartbeat. Most frightening was the electric stimulator machine. This is a device that is supposed to send a current into your muscle, jolting it to make it heal faster. It is obviously important that it be of high quality, but the Kiev team's stimulator, with its czarist-era look, had a basic flaw—the knob controlling the voltage level didn't work. There was no way to read what charge you were getting. It was trial and error, and being unaware, I got on there once and took a payload for a calf injury that almost shot me out of the room.

When anyone went in for treatment we took bets on whether he'd return with smoke coming out of his wound. There was many a time we wanted to put Teapot on the stimulator and turn her up full blast.

Already, just two weeks into camp, I was beginning to have nightmares of him barking out endless commands on every exercise imaginable. One of my purposes here was to see how I measured up physically against Soviet athletes. I wanted to compare myself in every way with the Soviets and find out what there was in the human dimension that separated us.

Physical makeup was the first test, and in this I expected to measure up well, firstly because I had done well all my life, and secondly because I had seen these guys. They had the gulag look, sunken, drained. There was no shine to their hair, they had blanks in their eyes, and they ate record grease in their food. They projected not energy but lassitude. As a full-blooded, sports-mad American, I know I looked in better condition, more healthy, gave off more energy.

But I soon found new meaning in the cliché about looks being deceiving. I could barely keep up. These guys (though the team was based in the Ukraine, they were mostly Russian) were primed like thoroughbreds. The conventional image in the West of the Soviet athlete was man turned machine. The image, I soon discovered, was close to the reality. They were tireless in a mechanized way, expressionless, their motors on automatic pilot. They had so much spring in their bodies yet they didn't drink water during their training. I'd always been taught that you drink a lot of fluids during and after, but these guys went about their work with the forbearance and stoicism of camels.

During the second week we had the beach run. The sun screeched that day. It must have been the hottest day of the year. When they bussed us to the waterfront, I thought the idea might be to get a little swimming, tanning, relaxation. But soon we were barefoot on the searing sand, running great wide-arc laps without me knowing how many were still to come. Early, very early, my body, my instincts, everything in me was telling me I was not going to make it. I had started in the middle of the pack but was already beginning to fade. I looked behind me and saw only two members of the team. They were far behind, but they were the goalkeepers and they didn't count. They weren't expected to train as the others. "Oh to be a goalie," I was thinking in my breathless misery. "How do they rate?" In the U.S., goalies had to train about as hard as the others, but at this camp they mainly played tennis. Anatole Tarasov, the father of Russian hockey, had made tennis an obligatory training art for goalies so as to develop hand-eye coordination. Tarasov made his most famous goaltender, Vladislav Tretiak, carry a tennis ball around with him at all times. Once when the team was training in the Black Sea, Tretiak was swimming with the others and Tarasov upbraided him, demanding, "Where's your tennis ball?" Tretiak emerged from the water with a "you've-got-to-be-kidding" look on his face, whereupon Tarasov had him sew a pocket on his trunks so he could carry a tennis ball—even at the beach. Tretiak, though, had to train just as hard as anyone else on the team. That was the difference. He didn't slack off like these two overweight goalies, way behind me on the beach, moving like turtles.

My feet were beginning to blister against the smoldering sand now and grains were rubbing against an open wound. The Russian players, needless to say, were moving along in an easy rhythm, like the waves on the sea. Occasionally a player would half-haughtily look over at me, it being obvious from the expression that he realized my anguish.

I remembered someone telling me about Igor Larionov's prediction—"Hartje won't last a month." And from his promontory where he inspected the proceedings I could detect Teapot's dumb, puckish grin.

Good attitude, I told myself. Maintain a good attitude. The words came back to me now, and I reached for the best that was in me and pushed harder through the caldron of sand. Must have been ten miles, ten miles of running on flames. I forced myself, willed it, made my mind numb to the senses and in the end found myself right up there with the others. I'd made it, passed my first big test. Full of quiet self-congratulation, trying to camouflage the fact that I was on the edge of collapse, I ventured a look at the others. They were a coolish white, breathing easy, ready to do another ten.

Back at the camp I would have killed for some cold pop or juice instead of that kafir milk crap. Unlike at home, I couldn't run to the corner store and get a soda. There were no convenience stores, not even downtown. I couldn't pick up a phone and order a pizza. I couldn't throw a movie that I could understand into a VCR. It was the all-star break in the baseball season and I had no English newspapers, no sports page, to tell me how many players my hometown Twins had placed on the team. I still hadn't been able to get a call through to Nicole or my family.

On the way through the city center on the team bus, I was able to slip into the foreign-currency store where I stocked up on thirty dollars' worth of pop and juice. I gave the bus driver an apple juice and he was excited but didn't drink it himself. He tucked it away so he could give it to his daughter when he got home.

I couldn't allow myself to get so thirsty again at the dryland training sessions or at on-ice practices. I was arriving at the sessions too weak from the ones before, and once there I faced not just these superprimed athletes, but a different way of going about the game.

I prided myself on defensive skills, aggressive forechecking, racing into the other team's zone, knocking over a guy, and stealing the puck. With their highly technical skills though, the Russians geared most everything to offense. In our scrimmages, the team in possession of the puck was given free rein to organize its attack. Defenders would not fire in early as we did at Harvard to break up an attack at its inception. In the Soviet system, the team without the puck idled in the center zone as the opponents regrouped, circled, and weaved into formation.

The Russian game was also much more lateral. They moved laterally quickly, effortlessly. Just before they hit the opposing blueline they were apt to make myriad lateral shifts, throwing me way offsides.

Instead of concentrating on playing my game at my capacity I was trying to learn the new style. Besides the

scrimmages, there were drills that I had never seen before and there was no one to explain them to me in
English. So I had to watch and try to copy. I had to
think, then play. But you can't do that. In a high-speed
game like hockey, you can't be second-guessing yourself.
It left me another step behind athletes who were a step
ahead to begin with.

It was apparent that even in the best of condition,
neither I nor my teammates back home had the same
command of our bodies as these Russians. They would
fall to the ice and be up as if off a springboard. They
controlled a puck in their feet like jugglers with pins in
their hands. We had Ramil Yuldashev, the highest goal
scorer in the Soviet hockey league, on our team. He
was the master at gathering in a flying puck. He
seemed to attract it like radar, catching it no matter
what the speed in his skates and flipping it, with the
facility of a midfielder in soccer, up to the blade of his
stick.

The genesis of many of the skills seen in Soviet hockey
lay in soccer. Soccer players were the first to play hockey
in Russia a hundred years ago. In the St. Petersburg
winters the fields used by soccer teams froze over and
the teams took skates, sticks, and a ball and played their
own Russian brand of ice hockey. They used eleven players to a side as in soccer and played hockey in the style
of their summer sport: an overabundance of passes,
much lateral movement, quick transition game, a lot of
time organizing the attack, superior use of the feet. The
method contrasted with the more rugged, trolleybus,
up-and-down style developed on smaller rinks in Can-

ada and the U.S. So successful were the Russians in hockey that after changing to Western rules in 1946 they won the world amateur championship in their first attempt in 1954. In their first series with professionals in 1972, they beat Canada three times in eight tries. By the end of the 1970s they were recognized as number one in the world in the sport.

Today the soccer mentality still influences Soviet hockey. The hockey teams spend large amounts of training time playing soccer, thus helping develop quick shifts, pivoting ability, and overall superior use of their feet on the ice.

Compared to the Kiev players I felt like I was in cement overshoes. Since I was the new kid in town and an American at that, it was natural that they were taking a close look at me. I knew that what they were seeing wasn't much, but it was early and I wanted to let them know it. I found out how to say "it's early" in Russian and told one of them, "Eta rana."

Though they were sometimes quick to berate each other on the ice, choosing some priceless Russian obscenities, the occasional dirty look sufficed for me. The team, it was quickly apparent, was divided into two camps—kids and vets, with age twenty-three the dividing line. After meals in the dining room, the kids cleared off the dishes from their tables, the vets left theirs. On the team bus, the kids doubled up in seats at the back, the vets took double seaters to themselves up at the front.

The coaches did nothing to blur the division. In their eyes, seniority had earned the vets a special place, and thus they aimed more of their comments at the young. At the practice rink there was a feature you don't see in arenas back home—a coach's microphone alongside the boards. If you made a mistake, not only you but the entire team and anyone else in the arena heard about it. Bogdanov didn't use the microphone much but Teapot loved it. I'm glad I couldn't understand what he was saying half the time.

As I struggled with my training, with my loneliness, with no corner stores, with my inability to communicate, with my fear of not making the team, I was writing letters home every day and anxiously crossing off each day on the calendar as it passed, measuring the time until Christmas when I would have my first furlough and return home. I was disappointed that none of the players were making an effort to speak a bit of English to me. The fine player I sat next to in the dressing room, Dmitri Khristich, knew a lot of English, Doc told me. But in the first few weeks, I would never have known it. I was making an effort at Russian, they weren't reciprocating, and I was pissed.

But things began to change, beginning with a hot summer's weekend when most of the players left camp and I was left pretty much alone at the residence. These were the worst of times, the times when I had nothing to do but think. "I'd say I've done more thinking here than the rest of my life combined," I wrote my buddy Jon Engels. "I spend so much time in silence." Time would move so slowly when no one was around, and on this weekend day I sat on the steps writing yet another letter. Suddenly tears began to well up in my eyes and I decided, "Well, I think I'll just let them flow for a while."

At that moment, a young player, Alexei Traseukh, walked past and, noticing how down I was, came over. We had not exchanged a word since I arrived. But now he sat down next to me and in a quiet voice asked, "Okay . . . you okay?" I nodded, and he gripped my shoulder, wanting to say more but obviously unable. We sat for a while, and he asked me again if I was all right and then he moved away.

When the team returned and we were coming back from practice one day, I turned on a tape cassette of Pat Benatar. In a minute several players gathered around to listen. They liked it and came back to my room where I played others. They surprised me with their knowledge and appreciation of American singers and disdain for their own.

My music tapes turned out to be the icebreakers, something in common, something we could try to communicate about. I made tapes of some of their favorite artists and gave them to the players. At this time Yuri Shundrov, one of the goalies who trailed me in the beach run, began inviting me across the hall to his room. He wanted someone to drink champagne with. His was cheap Russian champagne and I don't like champagne and it was in violation of camp rules to drink, but I swished it back with him anyway. I wanted to build a relationship with the vets as well as the younger skaters. To this end I was happy that the doc kept inviting me to sit with him up front in the bus. It became my permanent seat, just two back of Bogdanov and Teapot.

Thirty-four-year-old Shundrov was divorced, but one time I went over to his room he had a new nineteen-year-old fiancée with him. Normally all women were barred from the base, but this was a special visitors' day. The goalie had no other place to live because when he got divorced, the state had taken away his apartment. With living quarters in such short supply in the Soviet Union, married couples got housing priority over single people. Once you lost your marriage, you lost your apartment. The penalty didn't seem to serve as much of a deterrent to divorce. The divorce rate was crowding 50 percent.

Shundrov was too distant in age to be a close companion. Sherayev, the team captain who had taken me for the spin around town, hadn't said a word to me since. But I sensed maybe I was gaining a Russian friend one day when we were out peddling bikes across the countryside. This was one of our training routines—a fifty-mile bike ride. With a modern ten speed, it wouldn't have been so taxing. But we had 1950 bikes with big tires, no gears, and seats made of wood. If you fell behind on these treks you really caught hell, and on this day my chain came off, sending me and the apparatus tumbling into a roadside crevice. I wasn't hurt, just enormously annoyed that I would be so far behind the others. They all were passing me now, barely paying heed to my plight. I was despairing when I heard someone pull over. It was Vasily Vasilenko, a young player I didn't know much about except for the fact that because he was such a Stallone fan, the players called him Rambo.

He jumped off his bike, steered me aside, grabbed my chain, and in about two minutes had me ready to ride again. I got on my bike, said, "Thanks, Rambo," and with a charge of adrenaline from the warmth in his eyes, sped away, catching the others in no time.

4

After hockey practice I left the dressing room and turned to start down the hall when I saw Anatole Khromov in the presence of a tall, slender lady, probably in her mid-twenties. Khromov nodded as I approached and gave the woman a friendly little push toward me.

"Hello, my name is Vika," she said warmly, half-embarrassed. "I happy to meet you."

I nodded, said hello.

"You American hockey player," she continued. "I like hockey. I like American hockey player."

Now it registered quickly. Khromov had kept his promise—a Russian girl for me.

The heavily perfumed Vika was in my face, really close. She would be happy to act as my guide and translator, she said—as well as do other things for me.

Though slim, she was proportionate and not unattractive. She wore long-heeled boots, tight, gunmetal gray cords, and a similarly colored angora sweater over a chalk-white blouse that matched her skin tone. Her prominent cheekbones sheltered dark, perfectly circular eyes saddened by pallid quarter-moons below them. Brown hair pulled straight off her forehead restored an alertness to a demeanor easily brightened by a trigger-quick smile.

We used to have girls around the Harvard team who we called "puck-f——ks." On first seeing Vika, I couldn't help making, fairly or unfairly, this comparison, particularly in light of Khromov's prologue on the airplane.

In a good-humored way she made it clear that she was, by arrangement, the team's girl for me. But she wanted me to know about a stipulation. She had told them she would only do this if upon seeing the American player she liked what she saw. Now, she said, obviously flattering me, that she was satisfied. "We will get along very well together."

As we chatted, I learned that besides being a hockey nut who attended all games and practices, Vika was a teacher of English in a local elementary school. Her English, excepting the missing articles, was impressive.

"So maybe we can get together soon and I can show you city," she said. "Would you be interested?"

Without sounding overly enthusiastic I agreed. Not having a car, I wondered about transportation until Vika informed me, as Khromov smugly looked on, that the team would supply a car and a driver.

Girl, car, chauffeur, and as I was to find out, all expenses paid. I guess Sokol Kiev thought a young American from the decadent West couldn't last an extended period without a woman. In Winnipeg Coach Bogdanov hadn't told me anything about this, nor had the Jets organization.

I decided I would tour around with her once or twice, then decide how the situation should be handled. The deal, as agreed upon with Bogdanov in Canada, was for no special treatment. But how could a Vika served up on a platter be considered as no special treatment?

I wondered about how my Soviet teammates would react. For them, cavorting with the opposite sex was strongly discouraged. Strict rules governed female companionship. At the base, wives and girlfriends were strictly prohibited. At the practice arena or after games, wives could only squeeze in a couple of minutes to talk before the team bus would pull away. It was as if the hockey brass had determined that a normal sex life for the players would be detrimental to their hockey performance.

The restrictions were the most severe in Moscow. In Kiev the Sokol boys, as they were sometimes referred to, would be given breaks of a day or more a couple of times a month to return to their homes. After a victory the coach would sometimes allow married players to spend the night with their families—but only after they had made the forty-five-minute ride back to the base and eaten the postgame meal. This meant they didn't get home much before midnight, then had to report back at seven in the morning.

The enforced celibacy was among the chief grievances of the reform-minded players. They wondered how freedom to see wives and families and, in the case of the bachelors, girls, could undermine hockey performance. In the NHL, they argued, players lived with their families or girlfriends, took several months vacation in the summer, and still played the sport as well, if not better, than the Soviets. Why couldn't Soviet players do the same?

This wasn't the Russian way, the Soviet hockey establishment countered. Severe discipline and training was what had given the Soviets the edge in the past and it must continue. Besides, Soviet players weren't prepared for the liberties enjoyed by the NHL players. Let them loose and the discipline that spelled success would deteriorate.

The legendary Tretiak asserted that it was the training system that helped make him the best. "I trained twenty-one years straight to be in fantastic condition at all times. I never missed one single practice in all this time, including the day I got married. Maybe this made the difference."

When a Western reporter interviewing Vladimir Yurzinov, a leading Soviet coach, cited the success of American and Canadian players who enjoyed a comparatively slack lifestyle, Yurzinov wasn't impressed: "Well, you give us your conditions, your number of ice rinks and equipment and facilities and money, and we'll give you our conditions, and then we'll see what level you'd be at with that training system you have."

Given all the material advantages in the West, Yurzinov felt that the only way the Soviets could make up the gap was by superior training and devotion to the game. For the hockey player it meant no family life, no development of the personality outside of hockey.

Igor Dmitriev, a coach with Moscow's Red Army team, compared hockey players to great painters. "The artist has to be locked up for a month or so to get in the frame of mind to produce his masterpiece," he said. "If hockey is to be treated as the creation of a masterpiece, one must live with, and in, hockey. One has to refuse everything else."

In my case they didn't seem to have a masterpiece in mind. I wasn't being refused everything else. Coming from the NHL orbit, certain exceptions, Vika being one of them, would be made.

It wasn't long after meeting Vika that I received a letter from Nicole. As slowly and unpredictably as the Soviet postal service operated, it was cause for celebration whenever something arrived. Here, though, ironically right after the Vika development, was a letter in which Nikki was clearly signaling her concern over my behavior. She enclosed a copy of a newspaper article that said that Hartje won't have time to find out about the women of Kiev because he'll be too busy training. Just in case I happened to miss this paragraph of the story, Nicole had underlined it in bright green ink.

Well, there was no way I was going to get her mind churning more by telling her about my guide. My intentions were honorable. Vika would be fine for some American guy coming over with a dalliance in mind. But I wasn't that American guy.

My teammates all knew Vika well. Very well, it seemed. At least one of them, I learned, had gone out with her for some time, and others appeared to be quite cozy with her. But I need not have worried about stepping on toes. Foremost in the minds of the Sokol boys was that I learn to appreciate Russian women. It was soon clear that, whatever shortcomings Soviet men have, one of them is not a lack of pride in their women. "Russian women—the best." I heard this line many times. The Soviets were curious about girls from the West, but the respect for their own ran deeper.

Like Khromov, like the doc, the Sokol players were dumbfounded that the idea of a fiancée back home was preventing me from experiencing the delights of their girls. My reticence was interpreted as an insult to their country. "Why you no like Russian girl?" I kept hearing. "Why you no like Russian girl?"

They had begun dropping into my room frequently now to listen to American music or to talk about my country. My room also became a favored location because the Sokol boys could drink or smoke in it with little fear of getting caught. On his occasional patrols, in another indication I was being treated differently, Teapot didn't include Hartje corner.

Among those taking advantage and coming by most often was the player who had saved me on the long-distance bike trek—Vasilenko. On the Sokol team he was America's fan number one. That the first American ever to play in Soviet elite hockey had just happened to land in Kiev was for him manna from heaven.

Rambo had turned his own room, which would later display an American flag, into a shrine to Sylvester Stallone—hence the Rambo appellation. War, power, American military might—these things were his passion. His favorite movie of all time was *Platoon*. He had watched the dubbed Russian version fifteen times. Of the American war machine he knew more than I or any of my American friends. Watching CNN's coverage of preparations for the Gulf War, Rambo would readily identify the make and names of helicopters, tanks, any type of hardware that came on the screen. He had collected a library of magazines and articles from abroad on the subject.

If Vasilenko had a posthockey dream it was to serve in the military—the American military. Though he realized this was rather impossible, living in America would do for starters. Among other things, there, he said, he could make sure one of his mother's biggest wishes was fulfilled—that of owning a microwave.

Vasilenko had been in the Sokol system as a junior, but the team managers didn't see enough of a future in him to protect him from the compulsory military draft. For hockey players of high promise, a farcical scheme was worked out wherein they spent a couple of months in the summers doing military-related work to fulfill the draft obligation.

His promise not quite high enough, Vasilenko had to serve the regular two years. Mostly he remembered the ice-cold showers. "I hardly learn anything," he said. "I spend most time on construction. I dig holes. Also I learn shoot guns."

Twenty-three and married, he was one of those pointy-featured Russians—pointy nose, pointy chin, pointy ears. He had become a big talent, second highest scorer on the team, but watching him I got the feeling that he was like so many other Russian players of grand skills. The technical excellence was there, but he lacked the passion for the game.

With the Soviet government, playing hockey was treated like a job. Hockey lives were ordered accordingly along an average laborer's eleven-month a year schedule. The players settled into the routine and went about their hockey like men on an assembly line. No passion for the work.

Vasilenko's early friendship, along with that of the doc, helped me enormously in making the transition to the new system. It was evident Vasilenko did a little PR work among the other players on my behalf, and as they got more friendly I gathered confidence. One afternoon when the schedule was slack and a few of the guys were hanging around drinking in my room I got bold enough to suggest we all go out to a bar for a few beers.

In Russian beer is "pee-vah." It is one of the first words I learned. The verb to drink is pronounced "pete." To my request, one of the Russians shouted, "Dav-eye, pete pee-va." ("Yeah, let's go for a beer.")

Rambo, myself, and a couple of others jumped into the car, opened a quart of vodka, and drained it en route. The only drinking I'd done in the city had been in the big restaurants, so I was keen on making my first trip to a Soviet bar.

"Vot tam," someone shouted after we'd driven around the hot city for a few minutes. "There it is."

I could see a line curling out from what looked to be a big, old-fashioned oil drum on wheels parked alongside a street. Big letters on the side of the tanker said "pee-vah" in the Cyrillic script. A hefty, perspiring babushka was pulling on a lever and moving the locals through the line like a drill sergeant. The sun poured down and the sweat from the babushka's brawn was forming a small pond in the dust below. She was refilling tumblers without washing them, and though they had long since lost their transparency, nobody seemed to care. As many women were in the line as men, and they emptied their glasses just as fast.

I was quietly cursing myself for having suggested this outing, but without discussion we lined up and took our turn with the rancid glasses. I closed my eyes as I emptied one, hoping my body wouldn't quiver.

One could also purchase big musty jars of the beer, and my teammates availed themselves of this opportunity. With four bucketfuls, we repaired to the woods nearby and made short work of them. My American friends who had been over here had warned me that the beer tasted like horse piss. I found it heavier and saltier than U.S. brew, but better than horse piss.

This oil-drum oasis that they called a bar, I determined upon further inquiry, was about the only bar in town—aside from the ones in the foreign hotels which were off-limits to the locals.

Not long after the bar stop, I was downtown with Vasilenko when he spotted a kiosk and came to a quick, happy halt. "Pee-vah!" he announced. "Vot pee-vah!" He bought ten large bottles, then took me to a park. As we sat there knocking them all back, I asked him, "Why are we doing this?" He gave me a puzzled look and in a matter-of-fact way said, "'Cause we found beer."

He found some of my ways strange, too. Most days at the base I'd find a few minutes for prayer and would get down on my knees beside the bed. In walked Vasilenko while I was in such a posture one day. "Why you on ground?" he asked, a startled look crossing his face. Raised under State atheism, he obviously didn't know as much about religion as he did about weapons.

My prayers didn't make the two-a-day workouts at training camp any easier. I wish Bogdanov had forewarned me that we were here not so much to play hockey as work out for the Soviet track team. With all the pounding, my shins began to ache. My legs felt loggy by the time we got to the ice for workouts, the result being that my usual spring was gone. This occurred while we were on the two-a-day workouts. When a notice went up on the board proclaiming a new three-a-day agenda, not only I but even my Red machine teammates, those guys who had handled the inferno run on the beach so placidly, registered dread.

They warned me how tough it would be, and so did the coach. Bogdanov, who had hardly said a word to me, came over and gave me a quick translation of what was on the notice sheet. Even though the news was bad, I felt good that he talked to me. At least he knew I was there.

The new day would start at 7:30 with twenty minutes of calisthenics followed by a ten-kilometer run. Heavy dryland training would follow for two hours, between eleven and one o'clock. Following lunch and a nap would come an intense two-hour on-ice workout.

The midday dryland training segment, something unheard of in NHL hockey camps, was the most trying. Among the softer exertions were sprints, high hurdles, and full-speed bike runs. A major segment was devoted to jumping exercises that were to help develop the quick and nimble feet that are so important to the Soviet game.

They had you hold a twenty-five-kilogram plate while doing kangaroo hops back and forth over a bar thirty times. The bar was about two feet high. Another program included five sets of a medley of kangaroo hops, bench-presses, sprints, slalom runs, and squats.

Not always Spartan in their training habits, the Sokol boys worked out a ploy to short-circuit another dryland training segment—the long-distance bike ride. The route was a huge oval of several miles. Bogdanov would position himself at one end, Teapot at the other. Along the far side, however, forest blocked their view, thus making a gambit possible. Every day a friend of Captain Sherayev and a few other veterans would show up on the back stretch of the route with a car the guys could hook onto at the fender. The automobile would pull the players effortlessly along the route, out of view of the gruesome twosome. The driver would then return and reposition himself for the next lap.

Most of the training was geared to leg development—power, springiness, quickness, lateral movement. Herein lay a fundamental difference between approaches in our game and the Soviet one. While we tended to put more emphasis on upper-body development, the Soviets concentrated on the lower half. Ours thusly became a more crushing physical game, theirs a more artistic finesse game.

Making the dryland training segment more trying was the condition of the track. It was an obsolete piece of heavy rubber matting with so many cracks, crevices, and separations that it looked like a road map. On good-weather days, we frequently stumbled over it. When it rained, the water would gather under and between the rubber and it was like running on a floating track. Spectacular wipeouts resulted, always occasioning laughter from spectators who sat in bleachers in a more crumbled condition than those at the Colosseum.

It was embarrassing. Besides having no ice rink at the base, club Sokol Kiev was so strapped for cash it couldn't even get a decent track to train on. That said, however, I still had to look at the results of the training. And having done that, I couldn't help but put some faith in it. It produced well-conditioned athletes who could pivot and dart and effortlessly weave, and keep doing it all day long.

Strangely, after we started the three-a-days I started to feel better. My system was kicking in and I was less and less tired. I was spending more time at each meal holding aloft my meat on the end of a fork to let the grease drip off. My per diem trips to the toilet had declined from eight to four. There were still times when my body felt deadened, but there were also astonishing surges, days when I showed them I belonged, days when I kicked ass for the American side.

Most extraordinary was an afternoon on the rubber track in the middle-distance runs. I'd always been reasonably fast at these lengths, but having finished low in other physical tests against the Soviets, I wasn't prepared for much better this time. But stunningly, I ran away from them in the four hundred meters, I came up a winner again in the eight hundred, and ended the day with some late overdrive for another victory in the thousand. The result: Hartje, with three firsts, left them wide-eyed.

Steroids, steroids, they cried jokingly. I fended off the cracks, felt great, felt reborn, but noticed in the aftermath a few blank looks, one in particular which really threw me because it was from the Soviet I thought would be the most excited—the doc. The doc said he wanted to see me back at the base. There, he gave me my first lesson in the Soviet "Kollektiv."

Socialist tradition requires that the individual ego be submerged in favor of group harmony. I had read this somewhere and given it no thought. Now the doc was sitting in my room telling me I had violated this principle. By brashly outdistancing the others, by demonstrating clear superiority in these events, I'd shown disdain for the collective. "Tod, you must show more restraint, not run ahead of the others like this." This from the doc, a guy who had denigrated the Soviet system in almost every conversation I had with him. He went to his room, brought back his dictionary, and pointed to a Russian word. It translated to "modesty."

To hear someone tell me to hold back, when for my whole life I was told to push as hard as I could and go for victory, was a bit of a jolt. How do you win that way? I was pissed. My one big day of triumph was ending with a lecture saying I should be careful about winning. The idea of the collective might have merit in some circumstances, but how could a society move ahead in hockey, in sport, in anything if its best talents were ordered to hold those talents in check, lest they offend the socialist brethren. Now I knew why there were no high-fives after someone scored a goal over here. You were supposed to skate away half-embarrassed.

I took off with the rest of the team to the sauna, a fine place to restore group harmony. Soviet players were religious about two things—their afternoon naps and their saunas. Unfailingly, unless the Sokol boys wanted to skip camp to go power drinking, they would sleep every day between two and four o'clock in the afternoon. Not being in the habit, I couldn't always adjust my personal clock to do this and occasionally tried to dissuade them. When I complained once that it was too beautiful outside to sleep, a player pulled out his schedule and pointed. "Look, it says right here. Sleep two to four."

Beyond the mandate of the schedule, however, the Russians were convinced they wouldn't be able to perform in the evening without the long nap. On a game day, the one thing you did not do was interrupt it.

The sauna they saw as a health-inducing, privileged tradition. It cleansed them, revitalized them, primed them. For the uninitiated though the Soviet sauna was an ordeal. Fred Shero, the late, strange coach of the Philadelphia Flyers, the guy they called Freddie the Fog, summed up his one and only Soviet sauna: "I've never gone through anything like it before. First there was a steam bath, then a dip in a cold pool, then they started feeding us vodka, and after that, more steam. Then they brought out the cognac. I thought we were finished so I started to put my clothes on when two guys suddenly grabbed me by the arms and took me over to the massage table. There they started pounding the hell out of my back and asking how it felt. Well, it hurt like hell, but I didn't have the nerve to tell them."

But the Fog, so called because he walked about in a professorial haze, didn't get the worst part—the tree-branch flogging. Instead of branches he got booze. For my first sauna, they belted me with piping hot branches, then pressed them into my back so hard they left welts.

In future I went in for the tame saunas, without the floggings. But even then, for the longest time I still couldn't see what they got out of them. Instead of making me feel more energetic, the day after I felt like all the energy was sucked out of me. And like Fred Shero, I found that the pounding your back took by the trainers was particularly painful.

It was while I was in the Soviet Union that I heard of the passing of Shero. His death did not go unnoticed in Soviet hockey circles because he had been one of the first American hockey teachers to show a real interest in the way the Russians played the game. That I knew so little about the collective approach, that we knew so little about this, about their unique training systems, and so on was due primarily to the closed nature of their society. But when their teams began to play abroad and make surprising conquests, we still showed little interest.

I learned, while their system was on its last legs, that in hockey, as in other sports, the Russians determined the way to win was through the scientific approach. What they did in hockey was take the game into a lab and thoroughly dissect it. They had determined that on the basis of natural ability, there wasn't much to differentiate leading athletes around the world. What counted therefore, what could turn the balance, was superior tactics and conditioning. In keeping, they developed the year-round training camp system where athletes were isolated and could give full concentration to their sport. They developed a series of sports institutes to study the game and develop coaches. They created hundreds of hockey schools for youth.

They'd taken up Western-style hockey following World War II on the orders of the Kremlin. Stalin's wish to demonstrate to the world the superiority of the communist system included sport, and the best way to demonstrate athletic preeminence was at the Olympic Games. Unlike in our system, sport in the Soviet Union became a government-ruled and financed endeavor in which the athlete's major motivation was not money but carrying his or her country's banner proudly.

For Stalin, nothing but gold medals would suffice. Preparation for the Olympics was controlled by the Kremlin. When the Soviet soccer team failed to win a gold medal at the country's Olympic debut in 1952, losing to Yugoslavia, the team manager was denounced at the Kremlin by none other than Lavrenty Beria, Stalin's savage chief of police. The Red Army club, of which the manager was coach, was disbanded for the rest of the season.

Vasily Stalin, the dictator's son, presided over hockey. Under intense pressure to win, Soviet players prepared for their first entry into international hockey at the world championships in 1953 in Switzerland. At the eleventh hour, however, the entry was withdrawn. The team's star, Vsevolod Bobrov, a wonderkind who in one season averaged almost three goals a game, was too injured to play. He returned the following year, the Soviets entered the world championships in Sweden and amazed the Western hockey world, conquering the Canadian amateurs, 7–2, to win the title. Two years later, the Soviets entered their first winter Olympics. The hockey team won the gold medal.

Their hockey genius, their ice doctor, their coach of so many of their early champions, was the pear-shaped Tarasov. His hockey Sparta emphasized all-around athleticism. He engaged his players in a number of sports and set them to weird training regimes for hockey preparation. Players would carry one another on their shoulders during practices. They skated around on one leg like figure skaters. They lived hockey and didn't mind then because it was a form of patriotism, and they were prepared to do anything to win for their country and their system.

Success only pushed Tarasov to experiment further. Noticing how in basketball teams used different formations—a two-one-two, a diamond-and-one, and the like—Tarasov said, why not hockey? Hockey had been stuck in its traditional format of three forwards and two skaters on defense forever. Getting hold of a Boston Celtics playbook, the Soviet hockey Buddha took it to his laboratory and came up with a new one-two-two system for hockey: a lone defenseman to always play back as a stopper, two rovers to go anywhere and two attacking forwards. He implemented the system in the sixties with some success but could never find suitable athletes for the taxing rover positions.

No such imagination was part of the North American

game. It developed, as Shero lamented, on an ad hoc basis, reliant on the natural abilities of the athletes. "When I played in the big leagues," Shero recalled, "I didn't know what I was supposed to be doing. Nobody told us anything except when to change lines. I remember once they put me on the power play for the first time and I asked the coach what system we were using. 'What do you mean, system?' he barked. 'Just get out there and play, for Christ's sakes.' "

Tarasov once took a Soviet junior team to Minnesota for training. Shero was only one of a few North Americans to go and watch them. Another was Herb Brooks. Fascinated by the drills and skills, Shero became as convinced as the Soviets were that "a multiplicity of passes determines the game." The Soviets, he discovered, passed the puck at least a hundred times more per game than NHL teams.

He became coach of the Flyers, an expansion team in 1968, and by 1974 he had brought them a Stanley Cup. After the victory, he hardly paused to celebrate before heading off to Moscow for an international hockey symposium. "I needed to know more about hockey and I believe the Russians know more about hockey than anyone else in the world." It was on this excursion that Freddie the Fog was pummeled in the sauna room and kayoed by the national drink. He returned to take Philadelphia to another cup victory the following year.

His Flyers were a violent team that frequently turned the game into gladiatorial combat. With some justification, critics said gangland warfare was as much responsible for the triumphs as Tarasovian techniques. But positional discipline, puck control, and short passes were features of his team that other NHL powers did not have.

The Fog said he owed his success to the Russians. I was here playing for them, doing something neither Shero nor anyone in North America had done. I hoped, as the memory of Shero was invoked, that some of the Russian hockey magic would rub off on me.

5

After countless aborted attempts, I discovered that Soviet technology—so advanced, the line went, that it produced the world's biggest microchip—was indeed capable of long distance telephoning to the United States. My first conversation with Nicole, coming six weeks after arrival, was a teary-eyed, maudlin outpouring of emotion in which I hid a lot of the truth of my condition.

I didn't want Nicole to know how lonely and isolated I felt, how much I feared not making the team. So I painted a positive picture. She was aware of my habit of exaggerating the plus side of anything, so I'm sure she gathered that all was not well in the republic of Ukraine. The important thing was that the call reconnected me with my real life. To be separated from your past, with not even a voice link, for that long was painful. After the call I felt so relieved, so light, happier than I'd been since I arrived.

I flew into breakfast the next morning, and after the obligatory fare, green peas and matching wieners, I was waiting in the lobby for training to begin when up walked the security guard—the same dick who on my first night in camp bellowed nonstop smelly Russian in my face while I tried to dial long distance.

This time I could tell that he was in a different frame of mind. He handed me a freshly cut rose and said simply, "This for you." I don't know why he did it, but though I wasn't in the habit of accepting flowers from men, I placed it in a glass in my room and kept it there long after its petals had wilted and fallen. Alongside it was a super picture of Nicole. With her raven black hair, dark eyes, hint of red in her cheeks, and great lines, she drew many an approving comment from the Sokol boys who came by. Their remarks tended to make me more longing, more homesick. But it wasn't long before they'd be cheering me up with stories about how some Russian girls they knew could make me forget about her really fast—if only I'd indulge.

Moments like these were needed to break the monotony. The relentless training routine was beginning to cast a dreary pall over the camp. We didn't know what day it was. It could have been Saturday. It could have been Tuesday. They were all the same. Every day, the identical regimen: Wake up, train, eat lousy food, rest; train, eat lousy food, rest; train, eat more lousy food, watch lousy movie, bed. In the intervals, I studied Russian, wrote letters, daydreamed, and wondered how these players could tolerate this lifestyle eleven months a year, every year.

It gave me pause in considering a sports career back home. Hockey was a body game. What did all the pro athletes do with their minds? What did they do in the great chunks of time they were off? The Sokol boys hadn't developed any other interests, but I don't think they were much different from the bulk of Western athletes. Their one-dimensional life shut off intellectual development.

Seeing my teammates provided the warning. None read books. They'd come to my room and hang out, do nothing but sit there. Most every night, they watched a movie. No matter how bad or banal, they watched the movie. One day Babar was the only thing on. They watched Babar.

Only a few, in particular two players who had prospects of playing in the NHL, took an interest in learning the English language and asked me to help them. Not too many American players with a Russian on their team would make an effort to learn Russian. Still, I expected more. Most of the Kiev players were keen on only one aspect of the English language—the swear words. Their own tongue offered a ton of varying blasphemous possibilities, but they loved the English language swear words, and to hear them use them, with their heavy Russian or Ukrainian accents, was hilarious. Among the printables, their favorite was "kiss my ass." In second place was "bitch."

When our assistant coach would yell out instructions through the PA system at practices, the guys would mutter, "Go screw your mother." As they got better in English, the rebuttal was "Kiss my ass, Teapot." Had the coach heard them, he wouldn't have known what they were saying anyway.

Given the tedium of life at the base, it was hardly surprising that the players leapt at every opportunity to get at the bottle. For the Sokol boys, going to a restaurant meant only one thing—getting pissed to the eyeballs. I would have thought that the restaurant food—or any alternative to the monotony offered by the malnutritionists at the baza—would be most welcome. But in all my trips to the restaurants with them, I never heard them mention the food. Like at the base, they gobbled it up like it was duty.

Actually, considering the modest reputation of Soviet cuisine, the food at the base was not so bad. The main drawback was the monotony—the same meat dish, the same fish dish, the same chicken dish every time. And there was never enough. I found myself eating all they served me, but always being hungry and losing pounds. The Russians would fill up with sugar. They put huge gobs of sugar in their tea or coffee or anything that would take it and they would eat huge desserts. I didn't like sugar.

The first time we escaped the base to go for lunch, we went to one of the state-owned restaurants—one of those cavernous, gloomy cockroach pits that feature about a hundred idle, poker-faced waiters each looking like he wandered in from the valley of the living dead.

The overall lugubrious effect was that of a Romanian morgue. Each waiter wore a tux with so much starch in it that you could hear a thwack if one of their pantlegs accidentally brushed against a table. Frequently half the restaurant would be empty for the duration of the meal—this while outside a long queue of despairing Soviets waited in the hope of getting their jaws into the food, dreadful as it happened to be.

It was a piece of theater of the Soviet absurd that owed itself to the utter laziness of the restaurant staff, a laziness prompted by an economic system that left the people without a scrap of incentive. The cooks and waiters were on secured, fixed wages so they didn't care. The restaurant didn't have to turn a profit, so its managers didn't care. Why bother serving a full house? The system in place was perhaps best summed by the Soviet worker's line, "We pretend to work, they pretend to pay us."

Our soup was a good borscht but the salad had a bit too much of a shimmer to it. It got me thinking of Chernobyl again. Then came an entree of bony, gray meat nestled in a limpid pond of green gravy. The dish wore a look that said, "If you eat me, you're crazy." I ate it, and it was right—I was crazy.

The idea, as I should have remembered from my first meal with Khromov, is that you first assassinate all taste buds with the vodka. My teammates did that—even though we had a two-hour scrimmage scheduled later in the afternoon. Having ordered two bottles of vodka between the four of them, they downed two-ounce shots in split second rapidity. A platoon of beers that they had brown-bagged into the restaurant from the car served as backup. I had a couple of those but only one shot of vodka. The limitation was on the advice of the players and I appreciated their concern. The last thing I needed was to show up at the rink shitfaced. The Sokol boys probably figured I had a hard enough time out there sober.

They wouldn't let me pay my share for the meal. As they explained it, I was their guest in the USSR and only they could pay. "When we in America, you pay."

As we were walking to the car the sun was shining, a breeze blowing, the players chattering, and I felt very much at home in their company. That evening at hockey practice, they skated like the wind, like they hadn't touched a drink in a month.

The Goodwill Games, which featured events primarily between the Soviets and the Americans, were later on television. Watching the high jump competition, I chanted "U.S.A.! U.S.A.!" When my guy cleared a height I'd pump my fist, and when the Russian competitor made it, my Soviet teammates would politely clap. The flavor in the room was friendly, but I could feel some rival passion. In the 800 meters, Meredith Rainey, a girl with whom I graduated at Harvard, started coming from behind. It wasn't a Soviet she was chasing, and when it looked like she might take the lead, the Russians in the room joined me in my cheering. They cheered louder than I did. Unfortunately she faded down the stretch.

The games were in Seattle, and a couple of nights later West Germany was playing the Soviets in the hockey competition. I could hear the American spectators in the arena pulling for the Germans. For some reason it annoyed me.

The gap between us was closing. During the Goodwill Games, Sergei Fedorov, a leading player with Tikhonov's Red Army, defected to play for the Detroit Red Wings. Fedorov, 21, had been the linemate of the flashy Alexander Mogilny, who defected a year earlier to join the Buffalo Sabres.

Given Fedorov's talent, his disappearance in Seattle constituted a serious blow to Soviet hockey. At the Sokol Kiev camp, however, no one was complaining. "Good for him," was the feeling. "And now Tod," they jokingly asked me, "when are you going to defect to the Soviet Union?"

As the doc pointed out, anyone escaping the clutches of the hated Tikhonov would find a degree of sympathy among fellow Soviet skaters. Tikhonov had become coach of both the Red Army and the Soviet national teams in 1977. The twin positions gave him sweeping powers, and when not able to attract players to Red Army by normal means, he used arm-twisting, blackmail, and other methods to build an extraordinary powerhouse, a dynasty unrivaled in modern sport. Red Army, which was the major supplier of talent to the national team, won the Soviet league championship twelve years in succession under Tikhonov, from 1978 through 1989.

Coaches like Bogdanov, who developed outstanding players in the provinces, saw them taken away by Tikhonov. The rest of the league became a farm system. With Army winning the title season upon season, fan interest dwindled significantly and attendance fell. At the same time, Tikhonov's Stalin-style treatment of players inspired the resentment that culminated in the rebellion by leading players. More and more players wanted to break from his system and go West.

For Bogdanov, Fedorov's taking off meant only good news—Red Army's power would be reduced in the coming season. Anything that diminished the strength of Moscow-based teams brought a glimmer to Bogdanov's eye. In the forty-five-year history of the Soviet hockey league, no provincial team had been able to win the championship and rarely had one occupied any of the top three places in the standings. Bogdanov's dream was to break with history and some day finish ahead of all four teams from the capital—Army, Dynamo, Spartak, and Wings.

He was favorably positioned compared to other regional pretenders to the crown because of Kiev's handsomeness and its more Western lean. Given a choice, young Soviet players would prefer Kiev over a Soviet city like Gorki or Chelyabinsk. There was no drafting system to govern the movement of Russian players and little in the way of any formal rules structure. Usually if a player grew up in or near the city of an elite league team he would move up through the junior system and eventually join it. But there was little to stop the player from being lured to other more attractive spots, Kiev being one of them.

A capital of old Russia, Kiev had a thousand year history as fascinating as almost any capital in Europe. Its hills along the Dnieper and old architecture gave it a charm, character, and warmth not found in other Soviet cities. Parks were abundant enough, and in the summer they filled up with seniors who played chess or checkers and looked very much at peace, enjoying life.

My girl Vika took me around the town—to museums, galleries, the zoo, the botanical gardens, the university, the old town, the opera house, the Ukrainian exhibition, the cathedrals of St. Sophia and of St. Cyril.

67

The sites were splendid but the city was bereft of spirit. An overlay of Soviet cultural and economic impoverishment sucked away its lifeblood. At a department store I saw Kievites lining up on four flights of stairs to get at a closet-sized room where they were selling a rarity—leather gloves.

At a hotel I bumped into a tourist who said, "No different here than the rest of the country. Soda's warm, coffee's cold."

Motivation could not be found on the faces of the people. Though the picture wasn't as bleak as the Western media chose to picture it, the state economy couldn't provide enough goods and the black market had to fill the gap. I got talking to a young man in front of a hotel and he explained how his living was selling T-shirts and hats and jeans. I told him he would probably do better over at the Hotel Salut where there were many more potential buyers. "I can't go there," he said. "I have an agreement with the Mafia. I can only sell in this area. This is my territory." He had to pay a certain percentage of his sales to the Mafia every month, he explained, or face the consequences.

As she escorted me, Vika was frank. Team management, she revealed, wanted intelligence on me from her. They wanted to know what I thought about everything. "They don't think you will stay," she said. "They don't think you can last." I worried that they'd come up with that impression from my performance on the ice. In truth, on some particularly bad days I had thought about bolting. I'd say to the guys, "This sucks, I'm getting outta here." But by the next morning I'd always changed my mind. I wasn't a quitter.

Vika didn't think I would last. She thought I was crazy to have undertaken this and reflected the sentiment of so many on the team when she said, "Everybody wants to leave this country. But you come. It's crazy." We were in one of the new co-op–style restaurants run on a private enterprise basis. You were required to pay an estimated amount of money before you sat down, and then if you overshot on your meal you'd make up the difference. The restaurant had a one-person toilet in the back, but the only wash sink in the place was at the front, meaning that one trip to the washroom required two trips. There were about fifteen tables for four, and if you arrived as a twosome chances were you'd be seated next to a couple of losers who could listen to your every word.

Vika wasn't trying to come on to me sexually, not now anyway, and this was good because I didn't want to get in an uncomfortable situation with her. As a guide, translator, companion, I needed her. I told her about Nicole, but couldn't assess whether she viewed this with the same degree of dismissiveness as my teammates.

Vika knew hockey, and I knew after talking to her that my stock was low and falling. The question How far? was answered when instead of sending me for dryland training one midday, management told me to go suit up for the farm team. The farm team was Kiev's second-division club, which was playing an exhibition game against Czechoslovakia that day.

Someone pointed me toward this B team's locker, and in a rather pissed frame of mind I entered what looked like a cross between a boiler room and a 1960 laundromat. It was a small square with broken benches, peeling paint, and laundry lines—laundry lines with drying uniforms, Soviet jockstraps, and other reeking clothes strung all over them. The stench almost knocked me over.

I sat amid the limp, cold Russian faces, saw one player taking a hacksaw to his oversize shin pad, another trying to curve his stick with a torched newspaper, and a third standing in the corner urinating into a floor drain. "Well, big shooter," I announced quietly to myself, "welcome to the big leagues."

The game was played at eleven o'clock in the morning before all of forty-three fans. Neither the coach nor anyone on the team spoke English, or knew me from a Martian. They pointed out who I was supposed to follow onto the ice and said not another word. A few times during the game I tried shouting instructions but realized no one had a clue what I was saying.

We were leading 1–0 and with only a couple seconds left we had a face-off in our zone. The puck came back to me as time ran out. In keeping with North American tradition which suggests that a goalie who scores a shutout be given the game puck, I picked up the "shaiba," as they called it, figuring I'd do the honor of presenting it to him. As I skated toward him, the double takes began. The players stopped and stared as I held out the puck to the goaltender. He looked bewildered. I was going to say something in Russian but figured I'd just confuse things further. So I extended my hand again, which only brought on a look of more bewilderment. I couldn't make out his Russian, but the expression on the goalie's face sort of said it all. "What do you want me to do, eat it?" I ended up taking the shaiba home myself.

I played well among the B bunch but was mad that they'd put me on the farm team to make my Russian hockey debut. Maybe, I optimistically conjectured, they wanted to break me into their system easily. When Alexei Kasatonov, the Red Army defenseman, went to play for the New Jersey Devils, the NHL team first sent him to play some games for their American league affiliate in Utica.

In a few days, I was back on the big-team lineup for its first exhibition against a more senior Czech team. Our coach wasn't taking this one seriously. In the morning he had us run ten kilometers. In the afternoon we did a thirty-mile bike ride. Hardly the proper preparation for a game in the early evening, and this, combined with the fact that I just received another heavy letter from Nicole before leaving for the arena, had me in less than peak form for the match.

My performance was hardly exemplary. We lost 4–2, and one of the goals against us could have been prevented had I made a better play. Even though I was out there with one of the team's strongest defenseman, Alexander Godyniuk, I was too nervous to play with any confidence.

Back on the bus, I read and reread Nikki's letter and was able to get my mind off what had just transpired. In the next exhibition, against Dynamo Minsk, we tied 2–2. I was on the ice when both our goals were scored and off when they scored against us. Bogdanov made no comment to me about this game, or the first one or my farm team performance. I suspected that he and others thought that I, being an American, should play a tougher, more aggressive style. Despite the advent of Gretzky and Lemieux, the Soviets' prevailing image of Canadian and American hockey players was of bullies. Although I didn't mind a good fight or a heavy hit, this type of game was not my style. And even if I did want to smash these guys, I don't know that I could have. They were too quick and agile to tee off on.

Before the regular season began, Sokol hosted the annual Kiev tournament, a five-team, low-key championship which, like the other preseason matches, attracted only a few hundred spectators and left you feeling you were in a scrimmage more than a game.

Two of the games were against clubs from Finland. Some Canadians were on these teams and they were your basic brickheads—big goons always looking to cause trouble. The game had hardly begun when they started hurling insults at the Soviets. "Nice teeth buddy!" a Canadian shouted at one of our guys. "You ever hear of toothpaste?"

"When's the last time you had a bath, dickhead?" yelled another.

I was getting a chuckle out of this, then suddenly remembered, "Heh!—these are my teammates." The Canadians kept up the boorish abuse the whole game—to the point where I was embarrassed to be a North American. Though my teammates couldn't understand what they were saying, I got the impression they were looking at me, thinking, "Friends of yours?"

Starting with these games in this, a tournament that

we won, our coaches got very serious. At the first team meeting after each game, Bogdanov gave performance ratings to each player in front of all the others. You got anywhere from a low of zero to a high of five.

For two of the games I couldn't make out the Russian in the meeting and sat there with my stone-dead, lobotomized look. The doc sat in, however, and after each of the sessions he came over to me and whispered in my ear, "You got a two."

For the other games, I could make out the coach's language myself. "Hartje—nul," Bogdanov announced. I quickly concluded that "nul" means the same in any language—the big zero. When Doc approached, I sadly waved him off.

Godyniuk, my defensive partner, got grades almost as embarrassing as mine. "I didn't think we played that bad," I told him. "Ah, Bogdanov," he responded with a dismissive wave of the hand. "Bogdanov nuts."

I hadn't been on the ice when the other teams did their damage, but neither had I participated in many of our scoring thrusts, and in Bogdanov's scheme of things, it's your offensive contribution that results in high grades. This was typical of the Soviet game, which emphasized offensive play in far greater degree than defensive.

I was suspicious of the fact too that the guy keeping book on the game was the assistant coach. None of us felt that Teapot knew much about hockey.

Basically though I knew I hadn't played well. Better than nul, but not much. I was lacking in confidence and in direction. I needed to do what Nicole said in her letter. I needed to get an attitude out there, get mad. That's when I played my best at Harvard, she said—when I got angry, so determined that my eyebrows slanted together, giving me a mean look.

"Don't lose sight of your dream," Nicole wrote me. "Fight through the tough parts. Get an attitude."

6

Alexander Godyniuk, my defense partner, would look at me and slam his fist repeatedly into the palm of his hand. "Vot tak. Vot tak," he would say. "Like that. Do it like that." What he meant was that it was about time I started plastering guys.

My early suspicion was proving correct. As the visiting American I was expected to be the bruiser, the man of might, a smart-bomb on ice. Rather than adapt to the Soviet style, which I expected might be required, they wanted me to stick to the Western stereotype.

Sasha (the Soviet short form for Alexander) was twenty one years old, six-foot-two, 205 pounds. In his cowboy boots, handsome sport jackets, and trench coats, he was one of the few team members who didn't dress like a Bulgarian refugee. When the visiting Canucks yelled, "Nice teeth, buddy!" they weren't aiming their barb at Godyniuk, whose ready smile revealed teeth as white as snow. He was thick of build, with oak trees for legs, but the most talked about feature of his anatomy was his instrument of sexuality. It was unusually prodigious. When teammates made reference to Godyniuk they would often, in lieu of invoking his name, simply draw their arms far apart in appreciation of its bounty.

He was jovial, loved American rock music, and was popular with the girls. His Western lean gave him a natural interest in cultivating a friendship with me, and he became my most eager language student. Our communication off the ice, however, was superior to what it was on. During the Kiev tournament, for example, we fouled up on a "switch" play. It cost us a goal and no doubt contributed to our nul rating from the coach.

The puck carrier, flanked by a linemate, was bearing down on Godyniuk. But he abruptly crossed behind his winger and veered toward me. In such situations at Harvard or in the NHL we would call out "switch" and Godyniuk would follow the puck carrier to my side. I would remain with the other winger.

As the play developed I instinctively yelled out "switch" to Sasha. He of course didn't have a clue what I was talking about. He knew "bitch" but not "switch." So he stayed on his side, leaving the puck carrier with an open gateway to the net.

The hitting game was of particular importance to Godyniuk. He was eyeing a career in the NHL, where they liked tough guys, and he fancied himself as a major league basher. He was a rarity among Soviet players in that he disliked the larger ice dimensions of their arenas. It was harder to catch opponents and knock them over on the bigger rinks, he said, than on the smaller ones in the NHL.

Godyniuk had little loyalty to the club. He was openly critical of Bogdanov and the Soviet system. Drafted by the Toronto Maple Leafs, he was one of many Soviet players who were trying to come to an arrangement with Moscow whereby they could get permission to leave. Some had more patience then others. In Godyniuk's case I could sense that I might soon be without a defense partner. Sasha would jump ship at the earliest opportunity.

His best friend on the team was Dmitri Khristich, the player who sat next to me in the dressing room. I was almost ready to give up on Khristich when, after six weeks, he still hadn't uttered a word to me—even though, as I found out, he knew as much English as anyone on the team. But overnight he changed his attitude and took me into his confidence. The next thing I knew he was barging through my corner-room passageway at three in the morning, half-pissed, two girls in tow.

I was asleep and heard a crashing on the balcony and pounding on the window. There, shining in the moonlight, was Khristich's big mug. He'd missed curfew by four hours. That was one violation. He'd been drinking heavily. That was another. And he was bringing in broads. That was a third. There was no way he could go through the front entrance or the guard would report him. His only alternative, given the layout of the camp, was via my strategic corner room.

"Tod," he shouted. "Need help. Open door. Need fucking help."

Sensing what was going on but not thinking at this point that he was with anyone, I climbed out of bed without a stitch on and staggered over to open the porch door. Swinging it wide, I was greeted by big ruby lips, by eyes the size of hubcaps and, casting my glance downward, by a skirt so short it could have been used as a headband. Not quite awake enough to be embarrassed, I muttered a sleepy "Holy shit" and reached for the curtain, whereupon Khristich thrust this babe and another young lady forward and in. I was quickly back under the covers before Dmitri, or "Dimer" (as in "creamer") as I called him, gave quick introductions.

"Spasiba Tod," he said. "Now I go party."

I couldn't help but wonder who the other girl was for when, minutes later, he returned with who else but superdong Sasha to borrow some music tapes for their merrymaking. They weren't worried about being caught. Teapot, they knew, would never rouse himself from his slumber to do a room check at this time.

The scene reminded me of high jinks at the Harvard dorm. I lay awake thinking, "Just like us. These guys are just like us."

If I didn't feel part of the team before, I felt so now. What Dimer did was a compliment. He'd shown me that he trusted me not to squeal.

Three hours later (in the meantime, they'd snuck the girls back out through my room), Khristich and Godyniuk were down for breakfast and the ten-kilometer run. They looked like they'd just had eight hours' sleep.

Like Sasha, Dimer was a fun-loving Russian around whom most of the socializing on the team pivoted. Always grinning, laughing, he had a big protruding forehead and a bit of a hockey-goon look, but the girls liked him anyway. In overall hockey ability, he was perhaps the most impressive on the club, and unlike Sasha, Dimer was a team guy. Sokol had taken him into its organization as a kid and developed his talent and he was thankful for it. The Washington Capitals had drafted him and were pulling strings trying to get him across the ocean, but Dimer wasn't going to move until all was okay with team officials and government authorities.

Since Khristich and Godyniuk were leaders on the team, Bogdanov was in no hurry to see them leave for the NHL. In its twenty-five-year history in the Soviet hockey league, Kiev's best finish was third place in 1985. For several years in the 1970s the team was mired in the division below the elite league, the first division. Bogdanov now had Godyniuk and Sherayev on defense and strong scoring potential up front with Yuldashev, the league's leading marksman, Khristich, the very talented Anatole Naida, and my friend Rambo (aka Vasilenko). Realistically, however, prospects weren't bright for more than another middle-of-the-pack finish.

Bogdanov had his eye on building for the future. I was only going to be here for a year and wondered what stake he could have in developing me. It was another fact that gave me pause.

After the Kiev tournament, Bogdanov took me aside. In a meeting with the team he had given evaluations of the performance of every player. He wanted me to know what was said and in English analyzed the team's deficiencies. In my case, he agreed with Godyniuk that I had to play more aggressively. He wanted more offense from

me and told me that I needed to work on quicker movement, faster skating. I was too heavy in the feet. Compared to the Russians, I thought, who wasn't?

But at least now I had some official word and knew
where I stood. Too bad it had taken him so long. Instead
of leaving me out to lunch in a foreign language in a
foreign environment for so long, I wished he'd done this
before.

Grim news came at the end of the meeting. The team
was going to Finland on an exhibition tour, but I would
stay at home and play for the farm team. Bogdanov said
that because I wasn't a Soviet citizen my tickets would
have to be paid for in dollars and the club wasn't prepared to do that. Also the team was having trouble getting clearance from the U.S. State Department for me to
travel with a Russian team. These reasons sounded fishy
to me. I mean, what kind of an operation can't afford to
pay for one flight in dollars? But after thinking about it
more, I concluded that if I were being demoted surely
Bogdanov would have told me outright.

When I got back to the base I found that—eureka!—
the mail had arrived: six letters at the same time. I was
like a kid in a candy store. Now I knew about Dad's golf
game (I could picture him making those three birds) and
I had the box scores on the Twins, news from the
Harvard gang, the thoughts of my brother at the Pentagon on the country marching off to war, and Nicole gear-
ing up for Michigan Law School. My umbilical cord
restored, I felt stronger.

The next day I had my first visit to a player's apartment. I shouldn't say player's apartment because the
apartment belonged to the parents of the player's wife.

I had been led to believe if you were an elite-division athlete in the Soviet Union you lived on a pedestal far above the level of the guy on the street. The system was equal poverty for all—except the elite. But here I was with Vasilenko, one of the leading scorers on the Sokol team and, though he was married, he still didn't have his own apartment. He and his twenty-year-old wife Natalia had to share a small three-room apartment with her parents. Unaware of the severity of the housing shortage, I asked him why he lived in such conditions. "You think I want live her parents?" he said.

The apartment's entrance was dark, crumbling, and smelly, with light bulbs hanging from long cords. Maintenance for this part of the building was the responsibility of the state. Inside the apartments, where individual owners had the responsibility, the upkeep was fastidious and every inch of space was maximized. The main decoration, as in almost all Soviet apartments I would visit, was a large, heavy rug covering almost the entire wall. This struck me as weird. They had no rug on the floor, but a beautiful one on the wall.

Also obligatory was an imposing, heavily lacquered wall unit. These behemoths, invariably too big and ponderous for the rooms into which they were squeezed, seemed nonetheless to serve as a status symbol in Soviet apartments. To be with-it, you had to have a monster wall board.

Vasilenko was as much interested in showing me his Soviet passport as he was the apartment. The passport had a picture of Sly Stallone in it, a U.S. Army patch, and a pic from the movie *Platoon*.

The cramped quarters, the realization that a married

couple couldn't get a place to live on their own—even though in this case they had enough money to buy one—was one in the limitless number of lessons I would get in the USSR on how spoiled we are back home.

The house I grew up in was an average-size home in Minnesota and I tried to describe it as such to the Russian players. But as I enumerated the rooms, I suppose the house began to sound larger than it actually was, and with the Russians embellishing the story in the re-telling, it got bigger and bigger. Soon I was the owner of a forty-room mansion, a castle, Hartje Hotel. My being from America, the Sovs didn't want to believe that anything less could be the case. Many aspects of the visions of the United States they fashioned were biblical in their exaggeration. But compared to their own country I could hardly deny our's was the land of plenty.

I had been raised, as it applied to sport at least, in the era of excess. Accustomed to the profligate lifestyle of the multimillionaire Western athlete, I now sought to acclimatize myself to the frugal opposite. A first dose of the culture shock was administered the day Russian players visiting my room played music tapes. At the end of the tape, one of them instinctively looked for a pen. He then maneuvered the pen's point into the cassette sprocket and gingerly began to turn it counterclockwise. My first thought was that the player was just doodling for want of something better to do with his hands. When he kept going, I realized that he was manually rewinding the whole thing. I tried to impress upon him there were alternatives to this—a rewind button for example. "Just hit it and it will do it for you."

To illustrate I reached for the button. "No, no," he

said, taking it back for manual labor. "Waste energy, waste battery."

Their obsession with conservation extended to everything around. If you left a light on in a room around camp it was a federal offense. If you squandered hockey tape for sticks, the Russian frown would instantly appear.

Back home if the slightest rip appeared, we'd retape our whole stick, throwing the old stuff on the dressing room floor. The Russians would make one stick-blade's covering of tape last a month. If they broke a stick they would rescue all the tape from it and save it for a new one. They'd even save the tape that went on shin pads and the tape that held up hockey socks. It would take minutes, but they'd carefully remove and roll it up for another day.

Despite all the obvious lessons I was getting in thrift and making do without, I found myself getting thoroughly annoyed because my room didn't have a table lamp. How could I not have a table lamp? This was an outrage. Finally I went to maintenance and, while having no idea how to say table lamp in Russian, was able through some elaborate sketching to get the point across.

I waited and waited, getting increasingly pissed that the table lamp didn't appear. One day, miraculously, it was there, and my materialist mind was at last set at peace.

The Russians hadn't really had a chance to catch the gluttony bug yet. There weren't enough goods on the shelves to whet the appetite. But the greed potential was easily visible. A teammate got a pair of jeans from someone returning from the Goodwill Games, but he was furious because there wasn't a brand name on them. He brought them to me. "They don't have a name," he lamented. "What good are they?" I explained that they looked like perfectly good jeans and that labels were just labels. He never wore them.

With three weeks to go before the opening of the season we had upped our on-ice sessions to two a day. Having had the talk with Bogdanov, I was beginning to play more assertively and with confidence. I knocked heads, shot the puck more, and was on the receiving end of fewer dirty looks. But the team was moving off to Finland without me and I faced the prospect of life at the base with the B team. The only break was a quick trip to Moscow to sort out some visa problems.

On a rainy day there I lined up at the U.S. embassy and watched as the man in front of me, a non-American, was given a miserable time. He was trying to figure out what he could do with his briefcase, but the guard kept telling him to move and finally, very forcefully, ushered him outside. I followed with my briefcase and was sped through.

Among the masses on the broad sidewalks I was approached by a Russian who spoke good English, could tell I was American, and wanted to know if I had anything to trade. Unsuccessful there, he asked if I would write a letter to sponsor his brother to come to the U.S. Unsuccessful there, he asked what I was doing here. I told him I played hockey for Sokol Kiev. "Ah, the American Hartje. The first American to play for a Soviet team." He had read the newspaper stories about me and, now thrilled, wanted my autograph. He was successful there.

At the train station I met an official of the team who was to accompany me back to Kiev. We dined at the station in a restaurant where you didn't get to order. They brought everybody the same plate of food. Appetizers and drinks were available, however, with no one keeping track of amounts or numbers. It was an honor system. At the end, a waiter asked for your scorecard and you were expected to tell the truth.

On the buses a similar system was in effect. No driver took the money. You got on and paid a machine and received a ticket stub. The chances of an inspector being on board and catching the cheaters was about a hundred to one. But I didn't see anyone who didn't pay.

The idea that people were trusted to pay their fair share was admirable. In a pizza restaurant, the cashier turned her back on the open cash register and went into a back room several times. She didn't worry about theft. In my country, no one sane would do such a thing.

In Russian, I ordered what I thought were four pieces of pizza. In fact I had ordered four plates of pizza. Unaware of the faux pas, I took four pieces from the counter and moved away, whereupon the counter lady started shouting. I stood there feeling like an idiot and could hear the Russians at their tables talking about the "Amerikanski." When I figured out what had happened, that I was entitled to four platefuls, enough to feed a platoon, I embarrassingly picked them all up. My food piled a foot high, I slunk back to a corner, all eyes on me, feeling like the all-American gluttonous ignoramus.

Back from Moscow, we drove around Kiev to find a place to eat, but all restaurants were either full or closed. One encouraging sign I noticed was that for the first time I could remember there were no lineups for gas. I was subsequently informed that there was none—the city had run out.

Though I didn't have a bedmate as tutor like so many had recommended, I was making progress in the Russian language. My routine was to try and learn ten new words a day. With the help of a grammar book Vika had given me, I was able at least to clue myself in a bit on conjugations, declensions, and the like.

I was also getting help from Igor the hockey fanatic. Igor was the male equivalent of Vika. Twenty-six years old, married with one child, he was tall, slim, physically very strong, with his hair slicked back in a Pat Riley cut. The Kiev players had seen videotapes of Riley, the Knicks basketball coach with the straight-back, gel-rake look, and some sought to emulate him. It didn't work. With sneakers, argyle socks, gym shorts, and sallow complexions, the Pat Riley cuts didn't get the job done. It was geek city. If girls happened by, I ducked.

Igor the hockey fanatic was an employee of the Soviet army but somehow found the time to be my overly willing male slave. He would carry my bags all the time, open doors, get me sodas, arrange tickets, fetch my equipment. He held the NHL in awe, and the thought of an American player who was signed to an NHL club playing for Kiev absolutely thrilled him. Igor brought a collection of NHL hockey cards to camp one day and though I had no interest insisted that I take his doubles.

Like Vika, he was strong-willed and wouldn't take no for an answer. Later he presented me with an entire collection of pins and left me a note with them. "Dear friend Tod," it said. "Pins your present. For you pins. Friend you, Igor."

Leaving behind wife and child, Igor the hockey fanatic would arrive some days at the base at 7:30 in the morning, watch us do a 10K run for his first piece of excitement, then continue his chaperon act all day long. He rarely missed a practice.

At first I thought he was either certifiable or a Soviet military spy or both. Given the likes of Igor, Vika, and Vasilenko so often around me, I had occasional thoughts of being caught up in a KGB web. If it had not been for the cold war folding down so quickly in this period, there might have been good reason to be paranoid. But I always thought the spy game stuff was exaggerated and overrated to begin with.

With Igor, Vika, and the B squad I survived life at the base until the team returned from Finland. The guys invited me across the hall for an impromptu vodka bash to tell me about their 1–2–1 record, but as I had a game early the next day with the farm club I begged off after an hour. In the morning I ran, played the farm game at noon, then had a two-hour scrimmage with the team at night. In the evening Bogdanov held a team meeting at which he castigated almost every player. He went around to them, asking each to explain his performance. Clearly intimidated, the players would offer a whisper of a response that Bogdanov would then strongly rebut. "Pa-chee-moo?" Bogdanov would say. "Pa-che-moo?"

"Why? Why?" He would speak of the need for character. He kept repeating the word over and over. "Harakter, Harakter."

I continued playing with the B team, scoring points every game, as well as scrimmaging with the elite team. I wondered—did anyone know or care what this was doing to my body? Finally one day, the body stopped. I went on the ice and couldn't move, couldn't have made a peewee team. Everything I did was wrong. I missed my checks, I gave away the puck, I fanned a shot, I tripped over my own skates. At the end I didn't say a word to anyone, changed quickly, walked out of the arena into beautiful sunshine, and burst into tears.

I decided if I wasn't named to the starting lineup for the season and had to play for the farm team I would tell them to ram it. My lines were all prepared. First off, they'd put me on defense despite the fact I'm a forward. Second, I didn't get any coaching in this new position. Third, I didn't get to go to Finland and fight for a spot.

We moved into the start of September when our regular league season would begin without Bogdanov indicating the starting lineup. Everyone was still around, including nine defensemen—three more than necessary. The day before the regular season opener, we went to practice at the six-thousand–capacity sport palace where we would play all home games. We stepped on the ice and our skate blades sunk right through to the concrete. There was still fresh paint on the boards, a fact I discovered when I was bumped into them and came away with my pants a different color.

We packed it in after a while and took the long trip to our regular practice rink. None of the players grumbled.

Just another routine, absolutely normal, recurrent screwup.

I was looking over my shoulder all the time now, wondering when Bogdanov was going to tap me on it and point in the direction of the farm team locker. We practiced. Still no word. We slept. Still no word. I looked on the bulletin board. Still no word. In the afternoon, two hours before the season opener, a team meeting was called. I got there, looked around, and noticed there were fewer bodies than usual.

I did a quiet count again, confirming that many must have been given the heave, and began to feel real good inside. Bogdanov talked. I couldn't make out most of what he said, but after the meeting I went to Dmitri Khristich to fill me in.

Dimer's look did not have the excited glow I'd seen that night when he burst through my room with the two broads.

"You no play," he said.

7

Out of uniform I sat in the stands for the season opener, miserable. This was to have been my debut, my big moment—in one hundred years of Russian hockey, the first American to skate for them. Instead, without an explanation, the Sovs stuck me in the bleachers. Bogdanov didn't even have the decency to tell me personally. Did he think I had learned the entire Russian language in two months and could understand him? What about Sherayev, the team captain? Given the novelty of the situation, one might think he'd have tried to explain what was going on.

The game itself was a bore-off. The attendance, if they included me, might have been a thousand. We played a team in spaghetti-colored uniforms called Aftomobilist Sverdlovsk. Sverdlovsk, I guessed correctly, was the name of the city and Aftomobilist (auto manufacturer) the moniker for the team. With me muttering "please end" throughout, we clobbered the carmakers, a habitually low-ranking team, by a score of 6–2.

Anatole Khromov had mentioned something to me about there being political hassles as a result of Fedorov's defection to the Detroit Red Wings. The intimation was that the defection left a lot of faces fried in Soviet hockey circles and that further cooperation with the NHL on exchange programs, such as the one involving me, had been put on hold. Possibly this had something to do with my not playing.

I clung to this hope as I wrestled with sleep after opening night and again in the morning when they woke me up early and sent me out for jogging and weightlifting with a bunch of fringe players. Had I made the team, or was I not good enough, or was I a victim of a political controversy?

The next game, which we tied 1–1, I sat out again and immediately made up my mind to confront Bogdanov. I didn't come all the way to the Soviet Union to watch hockey games. I was convinced I could play with these guys. Instead of sitting back and letting events control me, I had to start making things happen myself.

I'd had these braver notions before, only to wake up the following morning to find them diluted. This time however, the nerve was still up and I walked straight into Bogdanov's office. When I was all set to lay it on the line he disarmed me with a big smile and a rush of congeniality.

He was "so happy to see me" and so pleased with how I was getting along with everyone on the team. He explained, without being too specific, that there were difficulties resulting from the Fedorov controversy. "But these problems will be taken care of soon. You will play. Yes, you will play."

I pointed out how I had been a forward all my life and didn't really like playing defense. "No problem," said Bogdanov. "You can play there. We will move you to center." Additional good news was that instead of languishing at the base with the subs, I'd be going with the team on its next road trip.

Relieved, wondering why Bogdanov never volunteered information like this himself, I packed my bags for another household name on the Soviet hockey circuit—the city of Ust-Kamenogorsk. The name of the team we would be playing was Torpedo Ust-Kamenogorsk. I hoped to be able to pronounce it by the time I got there. My friends back home, I thought, would get a kick out of some of these red-hot Soviet league rivalries: How about Aftomobilist Sverdlovsk vs. Torpedo Ust-Kamenogorsk. Laugh guys, but on a given day these teams could probably beat the Boston Bruins or Chicago Blackhawks.

Before we left for Ust, Yuri Shundrov, our goalie, got married. He went to his wedding ceremony at noon and was back at hockey practice at five. The coaches didn't see fit to give him a day off. He had a wedding night of a thousand pucks.

Only extraordinary circumstances resulted in leaves from the base, and nuptials wasn't considered one of them. The case of Shundrov wasn't unique in the Soviet hockey league. In 1971 goalie Tretiak asked for a day off to get married. He was refused. A few months later, he asked again and was refused again. It would interrupt his training schedule, he was told. A day to tie the knot would somehow make the great Tretiak less capable of playing goal. Following Tarasov's retirement, the goalie was finally permitted to wed by his new coach, the fantastic scorer of old, Bobrov. But Bobrov's more lenient approach to discipline was subsequently cited as a major factor in the Soviets' failure to win the first dramatic hockey confrontation with Canada—the 1972 series. During the series Bobrov took the extraordinary step of allowing his players to spend some nights with their families. "Bobrov was soft," allowed the happily married Tretiak. "If Tarasov had been there I think it would have been a different outcome."

After Shundrov's marriage, which only two members of the team attended, I was approached by teammate Alexander Kuzminski. At eighteen, Kuzy, as I came to call him, was the youngest on the team. In class and in smarts, he was a cut above the Soviet average. A silver-star winner in school for academic performance, he was polite to others and showed respect. Next to Dimer, his English was the best on the team.

"Tod," said Kuzy, tapping me on the shoulder, "we have bizzness." Whenever he had something important to say to me, this was always Kuzy's intro line. "We have bizzness."

The bizzness was big. Kuzminski wanted to get married. He hadn't told anyone else on the team yet. He hadn't told his girlfriend Natasha. He was letting me in on it first.

I didn't consider him one of my closer acquaintances among the Sokol boys and I hadn't even met Natasha, so it was difficult to offer advice. I asked if he "had" to get married and he said "nyet" to that. I asked if he loved her and he said "da" to that. But why the rush, I asked. You're only eighteen. "Soviet people marry early," Kuzy countered. "Four or five of my friends, same age, married."

He seemed quite determined, so I wasn't about to dissuade him. I was flattered that he'd come to me first and could only figure that it was because I was engaged and going through the same thing. It was true that Soviets tended to marry younger, and since religion was so absent in the society, the matrimonial bond didn't mean so much. Getting a divorce was a simpler process and a less dishonorable one than in Western countries. If this marriage failed for Kuzy, he could always try another.

Kuzy wanted me to be his marriage counselor. Godyniuk wanted me as English teacher. For Dimer I was an accomplice in crimes of the camp. And now Vasilenko was seeking me out. As we were beginning our first road trip of the season, the question of hotel roommates arose. Vasilenko took the unusual step of going to the coach and asking to room with me. Bogdanov gave the okay and I did too, figuring Rambo was as good a choice as any.

Since arriving in the Soviet Union I'd been trying to do as the Soviets do. Instead of bringing in a foreign car, I was traveling in Soviet buses. I had turned down a lighter training regimen in favor of the Soviet one, and I was trying hard to learn the Russian language. Instead of buying supplies at stores for foreigners, I was eating Soviet food. Every day I made it down to the cafeteria and every day I survived.

Doing it the Russian way had its side benefits, one

being a stellar education into the absurd workings of communist-style socialism.

Showing up late at the cafeteria one day, I found that all that was left to eat was soup. "Okay," I said. "I'll take the soup."

Sounded simple enough, but it wasn't. At the socialist kitchen, everyone's role was slotted down to the most minuscule of tasks. For the soup course, one functionary was responsible for putting broth in the bowls while another was charged with adding the meat chunks.

When I showed up on this day only the broth functionary was present. Meat bin man was obviously dogging it somewhere. Though the broth and the meat troughs were right together, my soup could not be served. One socialist worker wasn't enough to do the job.

The broth functionary waited and waited until his partner finally arrived. Meat man leisurely made his way over to his bin, scooped some chicken into the broth, and five minutes after I arrived they had my socialist bowl of soup all ready.

My accumulating Russianness reached new heights on that first road trip to Ust-Kamenogorsk. I was issued a Soviet passport. Just like for the Sokol boys, I got a passport with picture, name, hammer and sickle—the whole communist shmeer.

The internal travel system in the Soviet Union required that citizens show their passport at each stop. The passport would allow me to travel fraudulently in the Soviet Union as a citizen instead of a foreigner. This meant Sokol Kiev could pay my way in rubles instead of dollars and save a fortune. It would also mean fewer logistical headaches. Foreigners have separate waiting rooms in airports, they buy tickets separately, they board separately.

If I was opposed to this true Red treatment, I didn't get much opportunity to voice it. At the airport, Bogdanov called me over and said, "This your passport." I said, what for? "We must pay in American if you not have one," he said. "This big problem for us."

When I looked in my passport I saw that they had changed my name. From Tod Dale Hartje, I had become Tod Daleovich Hartje. The "vich" is the common suffix on all male Russian middle names. Males take their fathers' first names as their second names and attach the "vich." Thus it's Mikhail Sergeyevich Gorbachev because Gorbachev's father was Sergei.

I was also given the fake title of master of physical culture. To retain amateur status in official Olympic circles, Soviet athletes have to be officially employed. So almost all of them are given the bogus master of physical culture title. It essentially means gym teacher, though virtually none of them act as such.

Tod Daleovich Hartje, master of physical culture, bearer of Soviet passport, hid his American passport and was told to be as unobtrusive as possible. "Follow me. No speak," Bogdanov said. The passport wasn't good enough on its own. I also had to try to look like a Soviet. It helped that I was paler since arriving in the Soviet Union, had lost weight, and knew how to suck in my cheeks in a look of immutable Russian glumness. I lacked a few gold caps for my teeth, but I did try to dress as hopelessly as possible, once even wearing the deadly dress shoes cum sweat suit combination.

My first test as Hartje the Russian impostor came at the Moscow airport on the transfer flight to Ust-Kamenogorsk. As we passed through the gate, our assistant coach ran our names by the attendant. As he read mine I lowered my head and whizzed past; I made it no problem and got a couple of high-fives from my teammates for having pulled it off.

On the flight to the republic of Kazakhstan where, not far from the Chinese frontier, Ust-Kamenogorsk is situated, a couple of the guys saw me writing in my diary and suggested I not bother putting anything down about the city we were about to land in. I asked what was so bad about the place. "Roads, air, food, buildings, car, people," one of the players said. "You live in this city for five years, you will die."

"No," disagreed another. "In one year, you finished."

Their endless list of negatives included the people, because the Kazakhs were not Russians. They were darker-skinned descendants of Mongol hordes who ravaged Russia in centuries past. The team viewed them as a lower breed.

The aerial voyage lasted about five hours, during which all there was to drink was water. The seats were jammed together, leaving an impossibly small amount of leg space. There was no safety demonstration, and passengers were up walking around even as the plane landed. At the airport we had to find the trailer that carried our luggage and get our bags off ourselves. I made it through the gates with my Russian passport again, and on the bus on the way to the city the players joked about whether we would be staying at the Sheraton, the Hyatt, or the Marriott.

Opening the door to my room, I was welcomed by cockroaches speeding across the wall like Iraqis retreating in the face of Desert Storm. The bed was a foot too short, there was no hot water, no bath, and the walls were so thin you could hear every Russian grunt from the couple staying in the next chamber. It was September 10. I couldn't sleep and kept turning on the light to read my August 10 newspaper and to ask myself what I was doing here.

Downstairs in the morning I bumped into the smiling doc who, sensing my mood, declared that I should be thrilled. "You historical citizen. First Amerikanski to play in Soviet league." When I told him things weren't going too well, he retreated to his usual response—"You need Russian girl. Russian girl make you happy." He continued yakking, and when Dimer Khristich saw me later he shook his head. "Doc crazy man," he said. "Why you listen that asshole? He try to tell everyone how play hockey. You only one who listen him."

After journeying the thousands of miles to Ust, I, the historical citizen, sat out my third game in succession. At least they put on a good show here. The Ust-Kamenagorskians packed the six-thousand–capacity rink and roared with every whack of the puck in a game in which we could only get a 3–3 tie. Though I sat out, bunches of fans approached me for autographs after the match. Outside the arena one group of Kazakh kids circled me like they'd never seen an American in their lives. When they finally approached me I spoke some Russian and they got more excited. One handed me a five-kopeck piece (less than one cent American), insisting that I keep it. The gesture moved me. Even five kopecks meant something to youngsters in these parts, and I wished I knew what the boy was thinking when he gave it to me. Searching my pockets for something in return, I came up with an American dollar bill. His eyes grew as big as saucers.

Back in Kiev at a practice, I spotted Khromov and told him this whole exchange agreement was bullshit. I'd come over here and worked hard in training for months and now they weren't even playing me. Khromov smiled. "Don't worry, political problem solved. You play next game."

I was still unclear whether the "political problem" was real or whether it was just an excuse to bench me. But all that mattered now was that I would play. The next game was against the Soviet Wings. I practiced with the big team, and when game day came I woke up feeling just as I always did on game days back home. The adrenaline pace was quickened, and I was alert and anxious and nervous. I had wondered whether the competitive spirit could be transferred so far and so freely. I had wondered whether I'd feel part of this team, it being a Soviet team.

The answers were surprisingly unambiguous. I wanted myself and Kuzy and Dimer and Sasha and Rambo and the rest of the Sokol boys to go out and clobber the Wings. I probably cared more about winning than my teammates did. I was brought up on it— the American winning-is-everything tradition. The Sokol boys, it appeared to me, had a different philosophy—losing is okay.

Game days were quiet. A short practice in the morning was followed by a lunch with a special treat—a big heap of black caviar, a Soviet luxury that I got quickly hooked on. Then we napped, had a team meeting, and went for the game-day walk—about half an hour around the camp grounds. Next came the obligatory tea and sweets. The Soviet players downed huge hunks of thick chocolate, which according to the team malnutritionist would provide energy through game time. Such a theory was prevalent in the West, but later studies had shown that the boost from sweets only lasted about an hour and was followed by a crash. I took it easy on the chocolate and at the rink before the game avoided the thick black coffee that the Soviet players also relished.

I received my uniform. My white jersey was so big it could have fit over a tank. I asked for a smaller size but was told that everyone got extra, extra, extra large. Mine came down to just below the knees. The material was so heavy it felt like chain mail. I discovered when doing my laundry (we did our own laundry on this team) that the enormous quantities of polyester in the sweater precluded all shrinkage possibilities. To tailor the Bunyanesque jerseys, the players used coins, big kopeck pieces around which they twisted wads of material, then taped.

Luckily I had my own sticks, shin pads, and other gear. As with the jerseys, everyone on the team was given the same oversize pads and oversize hockey gloves and oversize sticks. The dressing room turned carpentry shop as players sawed pads and gloves, trying to get them to fit their bodies. Like the farm team, they hung great gobs of smelly laundry in the room, and, not having modern blowtorches, employed burning newspapers to generate the heat that could curve their sticks.

I tried to imagine the great Gretzky doing his own hockey laundry, setting the Los Angeles *Times* on fire to curve his stick blade, tailoring his shin pads with a hacksaw, and taping nickels and quarters to his hockey jersey to make it fit.

The players were allotted three Russian-made sticks each and these were expected to last several games. They looked with considerable envy at my imported ones, more because of the label, which meant status, than the difference in quality.

While I was getting emotionally psyched up for the game, my teammates throughout the day maintained a downcast demeanor, as if they were preparing for a trip to the dentist. With one or two exceptions the emotional level was remarkably even-keeled. It was what the philosophy of the Soviet collective demanded and what hockey genius Papa Tarasov had taught. No individual was to stand apart from the others. In the 1970s, the outstanding player of his era, fireball forward Valery Kharlamov, was once denounced by Tarasov for blaming a teammate for not being in position. The puck carrier, Tarasov admonished Kharlamov, is the servant of the other players, not vice versa.

Somewhat paradoxically, while not emphasizing individuality, the Russians stressed initiative and offense. I'd read another Tarasov dictum on Soviet sport. "It is not possible to play a defensive game against a strong team and win, except perhaps once, by sheer luck. Because when you play a defensive game, you forfeit the main thing—initiative. And it is initiative that most often decides who will win."

Before the Wings game the dressing room was solemn. We had seen no film of the team we would oppose and there was no discussion of any special tactics to be employed. Captain Sherayev, as he had done for the exhibition games, gave just one exhortation. As we were getting up to go out on the ice, he shouted, "Daveye! Daveye! Daveye!" "Let's go! Let's go! Let's go!"

Skating around in the warm-up I occasionally glanced to the stands to catch spectators eyeing me and finger-pointing. There'd been considerable local press on my presence prior to the season opener, prompting me to think that their main reason for agreeing to having me here was as a promotional plus to attract fans to the games.

They put me on left wing on the fourth line. To the annoyance of many in the crowd I was benched for the entire first period. "Amerikanski! Amerikanski!" they chanted. Heading into the locker room at intermission, Bogdanov told me to get ready to play. "I've been getting ready two and half months," I felt like telling him.

The fever was rising, though, and when I stepped on the ice I was anything but an example of an even-keeled collectivist. I was as psyched as I had been in Boston, and within seconds whipped off a shot that almost snagged the corner. The fans were instantly behind me, cheering each time I touched the puck. "Daveye! Daveye! Daveye!"

After my near goal, I set one up but my linemate missed a clear shot. I belted one Wings player with a hit that made everyone take note, and it was only natural that I got sent off to the penalty box in my first period of action in Soviet hockey. It was for an innocent pull on the hip of an opponent with the end of my stick—something that happens a hundred times a game in the NHL without a call.

In the third period, score tied 3–3, we had a face-off in the Wings' zone. The puck went back to our defenseman and instinctively I headed for the goal. We call it crashing the net, and it's common to our game. But it's something that the Soviets don't do. They will fan out in a situation like that, looking to get open for some fancy passing. They don't realize that crashing the goal gives you an excellent chance to deflect in the shot or pick up a rebound.

As I headed in, the defenseman wound up and fired. I powered through someone and was just three or four feet in front of the goal when I felt the puck. It glanced off my hip and zipped into the net without the goaltender even budging. I was shocked, and hesitated momentarily, wanting to make sure they would count it.

When they did, when the light went on, I doublepumped, the crowd went crazy, and I collected the puck as a souvenir.

Goal! Tod Daleovich Hartje! Teammates whacked me on the helmet; Bogdanov slapped me on the shoulder; the doc grabbed me by the arms and shook; a spectator ran to me at the bench with flowers and the Soviet fans cheered. They cheered like I was one of their own.

8

It would have been perfect to have scored the game-winner in my Soviet debut, but the Wings got two after my goal and beat "us" by a score of 5–4.

As I wrote in my log, though, so much good came out of this game. "I proved to myself that I can indeed play at this level. The game also reinforced in me the idea that patience can be a very strong ally. When I was sitting out games in the stands, I tried to turn it into a positive by watching and learning, and it worked. Right now I'm riding pretty high and I hope it's not downhill from here. I don't think it will be because I have a solid foundation under me."

I was so excited after the game—Soviet people milling around me and all—that I almost forgot our postgame jog. About the last thing you want to do immediately after a hockey game is go for a long jog. But with Sokol Kiev the postgame jog was a mandatory limbering-down exercise. More annoying was that it was done right there in the bowels of the arena while hangers-on and players' wives and kids and the likes of Igor the hockey fanatic stared on. Teapot made us do seven slow laps, constituting about twenty minutes of boredom which I, historical citizen, as well as all the other masters of physical culture on the team, could have done without.

Surprisingly, following the loss in the Wings game, the coach gave us a day off. I went downtown to bum around and met a young Soviet in the waiting line at the post office who bitched about how difficult it was to travel outside his country. Like almost every other Russian with whom I talked, this one said America was the best. I asked him why, and he said, "Because it is America."

Sensing that I wasn't sure of my whereabouts, he went far out of his way to make sure I found my way back to the base. "See you in America some day," I said as we parted. His response—a smile and both thumbs up.

At the base, or "baza," it was team picture day. The photographer, in the economizing tradition of his society, took two snaps.

I retired early that night, passing up a trip to a restaurant with a few of the team's more renowned power-drinkers. I didn't realize at first that the phrase "going to a restaurant" was the team euphemism for going out on a bender. I found out about it after one game when the coach saw me preparing to leave with a few of the others. He asked where I was heading. "Oh, just going to a restaurant," I said. The looks I got from my teammates, not to mention Bogdanov, set me to wondering about what I had done. Outside the players explained.

What I'd done essentially was tell the coach, "We're going out to get pissed, have a roaring good time, and violate the rules you set for us."

On the night I passed up the restaurant excursion, I was asleep when Dimer and a partying gang, several females included, stormed into my room and dragged me out of bed to a vodka blitz down the hall. They were starting to roll a movie there when Dimer leaned over, gave me a wink, and said it was too bad if I had finished my diary for today because the best was yet to come.

It soon became clear that he and Godyniuk had lined up one of the girls for me. Her name was Svete. She was leggy, well built, but had a face that could scare off a rhino. Not a timid type this one, she motioned while we were being introduced for me to come and sit in her lap. When I hesitated, she took it upon herself to come over and try to sit in my lap. "I like American boy," Svete said. "Kiss me, American boy. Kiss me."

Her approaches grew more assertive. "No cost you anything," Svete said. "First night, free for you. Only cigarettes give me. American cigarettes give me and I give you anything."

Godyniuk, Dimer, and the rest were getting quite a chuckle out of all this. They took me aside and asked me if I liked her. When I demurred, they laughed. "No worry, no worry," they said. "Padushka. Use padushka and everything okay."

I had been told about the old "padushka" gambit before. The word meant "pillow sack," and the context the Sovs were delightedly using it in was the equivalent of the greaser line in English, "She's all right if you put a bag over her head."

The story of Svete's behavior got passed around the camp, and the two of us were soon the butt of team jokes. Players would toss me a padushka. "Dis for you with Svete tonight."

I'd been away from America for a long time, and I could confess that even the Svetes of the world were starting to look okay. It had become apparent to me that an American in Kiev, especially an American athlete, could write his own ticket. Not just with the many pretty women, most of whom were excited by the prospect of meeting an American, but of course with the economy. With the plummeting value of the ruble, one dollar could get you about twenty of them. Twenty rubles— your one dollar—would purchase you a large meal with drinks. Five dollars could get you a suit or a good top-coat. For five hundred dollars, you could buy a brand-new Russian car.

My first major Soviet purchase was a pair of shoes. Cold weather was setting in, and I needed a heavy pair for slushing it in the winter. I went to the biggest shoe store I could find downtown. The store carried all of four selections—your choice of four different types of shoes. For each type there were about three hundred pairs in stock. This bulk selling, prevalent for a lot more items than shoes, tended to produce a rather uniform look on the streets. One afternoon in downtown Kiev I must have seen about a hundred women wearing the exact same print dress. Men walked around in identical sweaters—orange or blue in color, Styrofoam in fabric. Sweaters were considered dress wear with the guys on the team. For the first two or three games of the season, I showed up, as most players in the U.S. would, wearing

107

a sport jacket and tie. No one else did. Most wore their sweaters or sweat suits. I asked the coach about it. Looking at my shirt and tie, he said, "That's only NHL." I shipped most of my jackets and ties home.

The players and most Soviets generally preferred leather jackets—either real leather in the case of my more well-off teammates, or the fake shining vinyl stuff worn by most of the proletariat. Everyone loved the leather look. It was deemed the thing to wear, even though it was no longer fashionable in the West, and even though the Slav complexion, hair coloring, and body type didn't suit leather. They looked better in cloth.

At the shoe store, I splurged on a high-ankled leather pair with rubber soles for one dollar American. That my feet in these combat boots might look like a few thousand other Kievites didn't bother me. But when I, the American cool dresser to my teammates, showed up at the camp wearing them, it was a different story. The guys went ape-shit. Instantly recognizing the shoes as Russian, they thought I was pulling some kind of a joke. They'd respected me as a man of good taste. That I could go out and buy Soviet shoes was sacrilegious. The lines kept coming.

"What happened? You forget your real shoes in America?"

"Someone steal your American shoes?"

"Svete buy them for you, yes?"

Not everything Soviet was bad quality, but the players, most of whom had a sense of what was available in the West, loathed virtually every domestic product. If it was Soviet, it was inferior.

My parents, who had never been to the Soviet Union,

were coming over for a firsthand look, to see if the monster was all it had been made out to be and to see whether son Tod Daleovich was holding up. Never before had I been so anxious to see my folks.

It was a big month, because at the same time my parents would be here, the NHL's Minnesota North Stars were coming to Kiev. Minnesota was one of two NHL teams that were training and playing exhibitions in the Soviet Union. As fate would have it, my home state heroes, the North Stars, would play in Kiev for the first time in their history at the very moment I was there—playing for the other side.

For my parents I wanted to do it up as nicely as possible. It didn't take much effort, though, because the Soviets took over. I had been getting a sense of the generosity of spirit in these people since I arrived. With only a few exceptions they had been remarkably helpful, going far out of their way to assist me and make me feel welcome. But I still wasn't prepared for what they did for my parents.

Typical was Toma, the wife of Yuldashev. While having dinner at the Yuldashevs I had innocently mentioned my parents' pending visit. Before I left that evening, Toma was already making plans. She set a date for taking them to the ballet. She would get the tickets. She began making arrangements to host them for dinner, first making me vow ten times over that "I, Tod Hartje, promise to bring my parents to Toma's for dinner." She said she would drop whatever she was doing to help them when they arrived.

I went through the same scene with Vika, with Igor the hockey fanatic, and with others.

For their arrival, the team members arranged a fancy car to chauffeur them. We got one of the best hotel rooms available. During their first visit to the arena, a man I didn't even know that well came over and presented them with a gift of Ukrainian eggs and a flute that he had made himself. On the streets we got confused with directions. A Russian overheard us and not only offered help, but escorted us to the local tram, waited with us, and took out his monthly allotment of tickets, insisting we take three of them. On a walking tour of the city we poked our noses into a school yard. The master noticed and ended up giving us a guided tour. Most people we met during their ten days issued invitations for dinner. Almost every time my parents turned up at the arena for a game or practice they were presented with flowers or a gift of some kind.

I tried to imagine Americans putting themselves out like that for a visiting Soviet couple.

Of course, the Soviet Union being the Soviet Union, not everything went smoothly. After one long day, my parents returned to their hotel hungry, in anticipation of a big meal. They discovered that the hotel restaurants were closed Mondays, as were most other establishments in the city, and settled for peanuts and Pepsi. That same night their telephone wouldn't work and the TV broke down.

I'd never spent such long stretches of time talking to my parents as I did during the visit. My Soviet experience made me appreciate them more and was bringing me closer to them as well as other members of my family. I was growing up fast. We could talk about subjects we never got into before—international relations, economics, different peoples.

Were it not for some upsetting work by the inscrutable Bogdanov, their visit would have been just about perfect.

I was excited about playing against the North Stars. I had grown up watching them, and my dreams of playing in the NHL revolved around this team. Though I was now playing in the Soviet equivalent of the NHL, it did not signify to me that I was of NHL caliber. The game against the North Stars would be a test of that. The skills level was extraordinarily high in Soviet elite-division hockey, but the third-rate style of the circuit made it impossible to feel you were really in the big leagues. I mean, if image is everything, Soviet hockey teams were nothing. Empty stands, archaic equipment, no media hype, players who drove Ladas, names like Torpedo Ust-Kamenogorsk. Give me a breakski. This was a Madison Avenue nightmare.

With the ambience of gloom they played in, it did not seem possible that the Soviet teams were as good as NHL teams. And yet, there was something to defy that— the record. The record spoke volumes. In almost every series of matches between teams from the two leagues, the Soviet teams won. In many instances Soviet lineups were supplemented with strong players from other teams, but on the other hand the NHL had the advantage of having all these superseries on their home rinks.

The series between club teams began in 1976, when the NHL teams won only two of eight games, and continued almost every year thereafter. Fan interest in

North America was high. Hockey was about the only major team sport in which the communist giant and North American teams measured each other annually. The performance of the Russians in their 1972 debut against Canadian pros had captured the public imagination. Their ticktacktoe passing, their artistic, mannerly style, constituted a more aesthetic definition of the game, and in that they were so successful it was downright insulting to Western hockey fans, particularly Canadians. Canadians considered hockey their game, even though archives show the Russians were playing the game as early as they were.

The defeats increasingly frustrated NHLers, who turned up the violent side of their game to try to win via intimidation. By the end of the 1970s it was evident however that the alley-fighting approach was not going to work. Hockey communist-style reached a pinnacle when in the 1979 Challenge Series in New York the Russians crushed the NHL stars 6–0.

The Soviets were the undisputed champions of the world. "What this series should do," said Harry Sinden, the Boston manager who coached the 1972 Canadian team, "is bring recognition to Soviet hockey for what it has done—and that's to produce the world's best hockey players."

After yet more defeats, the Montreal Canadiens goalie Ken Dryden wrote that a turning point had been reached. "There can be no illusion now. We have followed the path of our game to its end. We have discovered its limits. . . . The Soviets have found the answer to our game and taken it apart. We are left with only wishful thinking."

The Red ascendancy was interrupted with the U.S. miracle at Lake Placid in 1980, but a year later the Soviets returned to form, winning the world championships and, more impressively, beating Team Canada in the Canada Cup tournament by a humiliating 8–1.

The results in team competitions reflected the trend. The Russians sent over Red Army, Dynamo Moscow, Spartak, and the Soviet Wings. Occasionally NHL teams would get the better of one of them, but never enough to win a series. Into the 1980s, however, North American hockey began to change to a swifter, cleaner, more European style that was once a hallmark of the old Montreal Canadiens and was now reborn again with the Gretzky-led Edmonton Oilers and their four Stanley Cup triumphs. The NHL was showing it had learned from the beatings by the Soviets.

During this same time Soviet hockey fell into a period of relative decline, and in the late 1980s they lost the big matchup with the West, the 1987 Canada Cup.

The increasing frequency of competitions between the two hockey systems reached the point where exchanges such as the one with the Winnipeg Jets were introduced and where NHL teams began sending their clubs to the USSR to hold training camps there. The Calgary Flames and Washington Capitals came to Moscow and other Soviet cities in 1989. In the battle of the NHL champions and the Soviet league winners, the Flames lost to Red Army. But Washington and Calgary had the better combined record in the exhibition games, the result constituting the first time that NHL teams had won such a matchup.

In addition to the Minnesota North Stars, 1990 also

saw the arrival of the Montreal Canadiens, who instead of trying to understand the difficulties the Soviet Union was going through, spent most of their time whining about the food and hotel rooms and not getting first-class treatment.

When the North Stars, who showed more class on their tour, arrived in Kiev, I couldn't help but feel strange. Before Soviet league games the teams stand side by side in the tunnel waiting to go on the ice. For minutes, I stood there in a Soviet uniform right next to my fellow Americans.

Brian Propp, the high-scoring NHL veteran, looked over. "I've heard about you. What the hell are you doing?"

"I've been asking myself that question for two and a half months," I said. I joked with some of the players for a couple of minutes, noticing all the while that Neil Broten, the veteran who had played on our 1980 gold medal team, was looking straight ahead, stone-faced. He was obviously trying to come off as the superpatriot who dared not consort with "the enemy," lest he catch some disease. I guess he hadn't clued in to the fact that the cold war was over.

His look made me want to beat these guys. We were a mediocre Soviet league team. The North Stars were coming off grim times, but this was the season they would reach the Stanley Cup finals. Their arrival had brought a noticeable increase in the intensity level of our players. From its usual level of about two out of ten it was now pushing five. Any chance to show their skills in front of NHL managers got some of the juices flowing. In the past, when it was unthinkable that a Soviet skater would play in the NHL, there wasn't as much to shoot for. But in 1989 the exodus to the NHL had begun, and in 1990 it was continuing apace.

My teammates wanted to know who the Minnesota goons were. I explained to Sasha Godyniuk that the guy to stay away from was the North Stars' bad act, Basil McCrae. Sure enough, first time on the ice, Godyniuk runs into McCrae and a fight starts. Fortunately Bad Act Basil didn't get out of hand.

Early in the game it became pleasantly obvious to me that the North Stars couldn't skate with us or maneuver as well. Our guys wheeled and darted and passed the puck around the Minnesota players. My parents were in the stands, making it especially important for my pride that I do well. We built an early lead, with me assisting on two of our goals. Heading into the dressing room after the second period, I felt great. Coming out for the third, I was dumbfounded. Bogdanov had walked in and announced that Hartje would not play the final stanza. No reason. He just said he was benching me. With my parents in the stands, with the opposition my home-state heroes, he was benching me. What I had done wrong, I couldn't figure. Two assists. No goals scored by the other side while I was on the ice. No giveaways or bad penalties.

We went on to beat the North Stars, 5–0. I asked my parents to be objective and to tell me if there was anything I had shown in the first two periods that had warranted a benching. They couldn't understand either. "At least it tells me," my father said, "you're not getting any special treatment here."

Despite the third-period embarrassment, I felt good

about the score. It reminded me that the caliber of hockey I was involved in was as good as any. I overheard Propp talking to someone after the game. "We couldn't keep up with them," he said. "They were skating right past us." If I could crack the Sokol lineup, I knew now, then I could probably make the NHL.

When it was over the Minnesota players gawked disbelievingly as we went on our postgame corridor jog.

I had asked Winnipeg to have some sticks shipped over to me with Minnesota. When I went over to get them, I made the mistake of taking Vanya, our trainer, along. With an eye to extras, Vanya wanted to check out the North Stars' supplies. They allowed him to do so, but the scavenger hunt that followed left me sad and embarrassed. While the remaining few North Stars in the room looked on, Vanya, climbing up and down all over the place, picked up every scrap he could. He took waxy paper cups, used ones. He picked up small bits of tape lying on the floor, and water bottles. He took broken sticks and elastic bands for socks. We just beat them, 5–0, and he was doing this.

I should have known that would have happened. But I followed it with another diplomatic faux pas. I came walking back into our dressing with a sheath of new Western-made hockey sticks. My teammates converged on me, grabbing at them and demanding "Just one, just one." But they were all I would have until November and I couldn't give them away.

One of the sticks was a rightie, and since I shot from the left side it was therefore no good to me. I told the players one of them could have it, leaving them to decide who. The bargaining, I heard later, didn't go smoothly. Two of my Sokol teammates got in a brawl over it.

All the sticks had been bound tight in my locker when I left the room. When I returned the next day they were spread all over the floor. From their explanations it was obvious that my teammates hadn't meant any harm. They'd only wanted to feel the Western sticks. They'd only wanted to hold them in their hands for a while. Yuldashev went a step further. He'd written his name, in big magic-marker ink, on a couple of them. Just wanted to see his name on the sticks they use in the West, he explained. Just wanted to imagine, for a moment, he was there.

9

F ollowing the Minnesota game we suited up for a
league match. This time, I played one period, quite an
effective period, I thought, went to the dressing room,
and got the word from the coach: "Hartje—no play." I
sat out the remainder, embarrassed again—for myself,
for my parents in the stands.

"You're a rookie," I tried to remind myself. "Don't
put so much pressure on yourself. Expect to get treated
like all rookies. Keep the expectations down."

My parents were preparing to return to Minnesota,
and I was preparing to head in the other direction—on a
road trip to the closed city where they exiled Andrei
Sakharov—Gorki.

The night before my parents' flight out, Vika insisted
that they come for dinner. Owing to the kindness of other
Soviets, my folks had been booked almost every night
and unable to get to Vika's. They had to get up at four

the next morning to make their flight on time—and so had planned a quiet evening.

But they didn't know how insistent Soviets can be when the matter involves their hospitality. Vika was not the type to let you say no. Earlier she had made me go to her nephew's birthday party even though it was a private family affair and I had no business being there. As I had expected, she had been available as a voluntary aide to my parents for their entire ten days. She took them to the opera, got them back and forth to their hotel, sat with them at games, gave them gifts—she couldn't have been more kind.

Now she was upset, but I knew she'd get them to dinner somehow. On that last day she came to my practice, found out their whereabouts, caught up to them, and pleaded her case. My parents agreed, had a sumptuous dinner, and, on her insistence again, Vika escorted them to their hotel and made sure all arrangements were set for their departure in the morning.

She and so many other Soviets I met had such an enormous capacity to give. They lived in a society in which it was difficult to get by and in which collectivity as opposed to individualism was emphasized. These factors had rooted in the people a generosity of spirit you don't find elsewhere. In their treatment of foreigners I'm sure other motives sometimes prevailed, and I'm sure Vika had other motives as well. But I was seeing too much from too many Russians to believe it was only that.

Like most Soviets, Vika wasn't very religious, but one day out driving we passed a boy who had been hit by a car and was being treated at the side of an ambulance.

While I, the one with some religion, mumbled that I hoped he was all right, Vika twice made the sign of the cross and said a prayer for him.

She watched team practices by herself and then would leave by herself. When she had free time from her teaching she'd see to it that I got my haircuts, my passport pictures, and other needs taken care of. Some of the jobs required her going all over town and lining up for hours. One of the club's drivers would pick me up at the base and collect her at a designated metro stop, never at her apartment. One night when I was in Kiev with her and a driver wasn't available, we flagged down a taxi. I figured she would get off at her usual metro stop, but she came all the way to the camp with me, turned around, and made the forty-five-minute trip back to her home by bus. The guys on the team were convinced something was going on between us and wondered aloud when a Svete-Vika war was going to break out.

After my benchings in the previous two games I was relieved they included me on the road trip to Gorki. The city, which in the throes of all the changes taking place in the country was going back to its original name of Nizhni Novgorod, was uncharted territory for foreigners. No Westerner had visited it in half a century. Because of sensitive defense installations, it was declared off-limits to foreigners, as were many other Soviet cities. Gorki then took on more mysterious dimensions in 1981 when the Kremlin sent Sakharov into internal exile for the sin of speaking his mind. For whatever reason, Gorki, which in English means bitter, was the chosen place of banishment.

Perhaps because of its billing, but more likely because

of its look, the city, an industrial behemoth in central Russia, gave me the chills the moment I arrived. It was gray, depressed, covered in soot. The people wore dark colors and no one smiled. They hardly seemed to look at or acknowledge one another. The trees were short, with leaves that drooped in sadness, and the flowers in their large beds hung dead. Overgrown weeds, smashed watermelons, and litter lined the streets. Buses older than the seniors they carried barely made their way along the roads. Cars covered in dirt belched black clouds of exhaust.

The hockey arena was called the Palace of Sport. From the outside, it looked like a long-abandoned warehouse. Crumbling steps, cracked cement, smashed windows, and graffiti greeted the eye. Broken chairs and scraps of wood were strewn in the weeds outside. Adjacent to the building were acres of empty, brown scrubland on which sat a big rusting metal girder, a skeleton of a building that shouted death.

Inside the Palace of Sport the lines on the ice were painted crooked. In some spots the paint was just missing and you guessed where the line was to continue. The boards looked like they had barely survived a hurricane. They leaned, there were spaces between them, and in parts the paint had worn away. Behind the goals there was no Plexiglas, only netting. The ice maker, the Russian version of a Zamboni machine, was a big green army truck.

To get to the showers you had to leave the dressing room and walk through a public area. Big pillars in the middle of the locker room blocked the view of the guys sitting along one wall from the other. Hooks on the wall served as lockers. There was no hot water in the showers.

After checking into the hotel, I took a pastry from my bag. Speculating correctly that good food in Gorki would be scarce, I had brought along the treat, a beautiful cream cake with rose-colored icing.

I was just about to sink my jaws into it when I was called to go down the hall for something. Unable to find a clean spot for the pastry, I placed it on a towel on the seat of a chair. Two minutes later, when I got back, it was covered with bugs. Cockroaches and assorted other little insects feasted on it with such vigor you could almost hear them chewing. I sat on the edge of the bed and watched. Teammates came in the room and looked on. Soon we had a gallery. One player began to chuckle, others joined, and soon the whole place was howling.

The Hotel Gorki was not one of the Soviet Union's finest. In my bathroom, the toilet wobbled and bugs raced along rusted pipes into a filthy shower drain. In my chest of drawers, many drawers were missing. A big, lumpy sitting chair was originally just one color, but the effects of spilled food had turned it paisley. The floor was a rubber linoleum with a small, torn carpet caked in cabbage soup. No pictures hung from peeling blue-gray walls.

Meals were consistent with the quality of the rest of the place. For breakfast we ate powdery pale yellow eggs with a purply sausage that looked three years old. The bread and cheese were good, but the milk they served was sour and thick and warm and gooey. A dry ball of chicken with a half-inch-thick coating of grease sufficed for dinner along with soggy oat balls, cold beets, and french fries that were either burnt or raw. We ate this food—about half the quantity I was used to at home—with feather-light aluminum silverware that you felt would float away unless you held it down, and bowls and plates I'd last seen on "M*A*S*H." Back at the base I would get annoyed because everyone would rush away from the dinner table as soon as they finished—which was to say about ten minutes after they started. In Gorki I was delighted to rush off with the others and get within reach of my wobbly toilet.

After the meals we were supposed to feel in top shape to play hockey. Against Gorki at least you normally didn't have to play too well. This was a team, Torpedo Gorki, that perennially ranked low in the standings. Given any choice in the matter, good Soviet hockey players would avoid Gorki. It was a picture of neglect and defeat. It was the Soviet Union I had in mind before coming over here. Some of my teammates joked about the conditions with me. Others were ashamed and asked me not to write about them.

At the game, the locals came out, filling the smallish arena. It was heartening to see that sport could do here what it did elsewhere. The lugubrious street demeanor of the blue-collar Gorkians turned animated and passionate when the game began. Many chanted "Hartje, Hartje, Hartje." Unlike Bogdanov, they wanted me on the ice.

They saw their team lose that night, but they were accustomed to that. Defeat only made that rare occasion of victory better—and if it happened when one of the Moscow teams came to town it was something to savor

123

for years. The Gorki fans could still talk about the time a few years earlier when Red Army came to town and Torpedo Gorki beat them. Red Army, the repressive, always-conquering Kremlin team, was practically invincible in those years, going whole seasons losing only one or two games, and never losing at all to a provincial team. Just to come close to Army, the greatest dynasty in sport, was an accomplishment, but in that one game the Gorki goaltender was sensational. Gorki held a one-goal lead late into the last period, and the fans got so excited they climbed the netting behind the goals. Coach Tikhonov, sensing defeat, went to an extreme he was always loathe to try. He pulled his goalie for an extra forward. In the NHL this is a routine feature of close games. Not in the Soviet Union. Even in Lake Placid, behind the Americans by one at the end, Tikhonov didn't do that. In Gorki, he tried—and it didn't work. Gorki celebrated for weeks.

Since entering the elite Soviet league in 1954, the Soviet motor city had only one glory year. It came in the 1960–61 season when the team finished second, cracking the top three for the only time in its history. Then, too, the story was the hot goalie, a strange man, as many goalies are, named Viktor Konavalenko. His performance in Gorki's glory season was so good it earned him a berth on the Soviet all-stars, the national team. Most players who made it there joined a Moscow team, but Konavalenko resisted the enormous pressures and remained a Gorki patriot, playing out his career in his grubby home city.

The Gorki goalie was a central figure in some of great Soviet-Czech ice battles of the late 1960s. The Czechs, their country occupied by the Red Army since the 1940s, got an opportunity at the world amateur hockey championships every year to put their loathing on the line. Throughout the 1960s the Czechs had come close but never toppled the Russians in the championships. In studying the Russian team, the Czech coaches knew that Konovalenko, a nervous goaltender, worked in a rhythm, and if you could break it, you could break him. At the 1968 Grenoble Olympics, the year the Russians invaded Czechoslovakia to put down the democratic uprising, Konovalenko was in his groove. On a technicality the Czech coaches provoked a game delay. They charged that the Soviet players did not have the required protectors on their skate blades. The delay and the resultant confusion had the desired effect. Konovalenko was thrown out of sync, his concentration lost. He allowed some easy goals, the Czechs skated to a glorious 5–4 triumph, and in Prague they celebrated.

By the time of my first visit to Gorki, Czechoslovakia had been set free by Mikhail Gorbachev, and he had started his own country well on the road to freedom. But you would have never known anything historic was happening in Gorki. While we stood in the hotel there, I picked up a book that talked about the victory of communism and how this was the best thing that could have happened to the Soviet people. The doc was looking over my shoulder. "We've seen this victory in this city, haven't we?"

Leaving the hotel was cause for celebration. But as we piled onto the bus, the manager came storming out the front door yelling that a towel was missing. We delayed departure in a losing effort to find the Hotel Gorki's

125

missing towel. Maybe the bugs had carted it off with my pastry.

I had been looking forward to road trips in the Soviet Union, but the Ust-Kamenogorsk–Gorki combination had drained my appetite. It wasn't just the cities, the food, the hotels, the trains, the dressing rooms, the planes. Added to it all was the regimentation mentality that governed our every movement. Everything was rush, rush, rush. There was far more than enough time in the day for everything we had to do, but we rushed from one spot to another in order to have extra time to do nothing. I remember my college road trips as being quiet days with time for reflection. We would bus to the site, rest in the hotel, watch some TV, hang out, order a pizza, go to bed. The next day was game day and we didn't have to do anything until 5 P.M. when we left for the rink. The morning skate was optional.

But punctuality and schedule-mania seemed bred into the Russian player's bone. The Kiev players couldn't wait until the bus came to a halt before lining up in the aisle to get off. If someone wasn't moving they'd shout at him to get going. Then they'd rush into the lobby, only to stand there for an hour. The morning of a game you like to relax, especially on a road trip, when chances are you've arrived late the night before. On road trips in the Soviet Union they made you get up early so everyone could stand in single file and be counted. Attendance taken, a long walk was then mandatory before rushing off to breakfast and the mandatory 9 A.M. skate. A schedule mapped out every other minute of the day, including nap hours, leaving no time for—I hesitate to use the word—sight-seeing. Traveling

126

was an experience. On a regular passenger airline, Gorki is less than a three-hour flight from Kiev. Our return trip home took us eighteen hours.

We left immediately after the game in order to catch a train to Moscow. The train compartment was about two hundred degrees and I was jammed in a cabin with three others. Arriving in Moscow at six in the morning, we then went straight from the railroad station to the airport for a flight at noon. In order to save time we rushed on and off the bus. At the airport we began our five-hour wait in a room that allowed in a cold wind. We shivered there a couple of hours before we were permitted to check our bags. Then we got to our proper waiting room where the hours spent were warmer.

Though the demand for food and coffee is always tremendous at these airports, the snack counters are closed more often than not. When they are open, the lines are endless. Most everything is premade, but the people behind the counters have no incentive to move. Half of them work while the others just sort of hang out. On the way back from Gorki, the snack bars were closed throughout all the early hours and we had nothing.

We went out on the tarmac and waited for a bus to take us to our plane. As usual, when we got to the aircraft, we couldn't board right away. A cold rain began, and we took cover under the fuselage.

Back in Kiev, finally back in Kiev, we were given a light day to recuperate from the Gorki tour. Twenty-year-old forward Andrei Sidorov got the news that his expectant wife was in labor at the hospital. Instead of taking off for the hospital, Sidorov hung around the camp all day. I was unsure if the coach wouldn't give

127

him the leave or whether he just didn't care enough to go there. But he was excited about the baby's pending arrival, so I suspect he was denied leave. During this period, Kuzminski often expressed to me his worry that Bogdanov would not give him time off to get married and that he might have to postpone the whole thing.

The next day the coach delivered the news to Sidorov that his wife had the baby and all was well. Bogdanov didn't even do it in private. He walked in amid a bunch of players and announced the news.

I caught the coach after dinner one night and got him talking about my lack of ice time. Forwards on a hockey team have to score goals, he told me straightforwardly, and I hadn't been scoring goals. It was clear that he had little use for hard-checking skaters whose main strength was defense. If you score, he noted in that conversation, poor defensive play is only a small problem. I had played parts of four games when we talked and had only the one goal. Never a naturally gifted scorer, I didn't expect to put in a ton of goals in my first crack at big-time hockey. How many rookies in the NHL score more than a few goals? How many would they score coming over to play their rookie season in the Soviet Union?

One of the points-rating systems that the coach employed underrated fine defensive play and downgraded assists. Whereas in our system, goals and assists are rated equally, Bogdanov awarded five points for a goal, three for an assist. Moreover assists were given infrequently. Two assists per goal, given frequently in the NHL, is very rare in the Soviet league.

The summary effect of his system was to honor scoring at the expense of everything else. You could score, for example, two goals, and get ten points from Bogdanov. During the same period you could play abysmally defensively, be on the ice for nine goals scored against your team, and still end up in the positive column—a plus one, your two goals scored outweighing your nine against.

I could rationalize my difficulties, but the bottom line was that Bogdanov's philosophy of hockey did not mesh with mine and it was going to be a long year. I began to think more in terms of what my parents and others had told me—that hockey was but one of the reasons I was here, that what I'd learn in hockey was important, but what I'd learn about life, Gorki being an example, was more important.

The players didn't talk to me about hockey so much. They were more interested in the United States, in girls, in drinking. Occasionally we would drink down in the parking lot in one of the cars. We were poking back some vodka there once when a couple of senior Soviets happened by. They had obviously come from one of the many vacation and rest homes in the area. They had a bottle too, saw us drinking, and joined the party. We shared our vodka. They shared their cognac. With virtually no public places in the city to drink other than the restaurants, why not a car bar?

Our nights off were usually big party nights, so much so that I could understand why Bogdanov was reluctant to schedule too many. Maybe the Soviet coaches had a point. If you ever gave these players the freedoms players have in the NHL, it might be too much for them to handle.

Following a 6–3 win in early October we had a free

night, and several of us stopped off at the Hotel Rus to stock up. We got two bottles of champagne, one bottle of vodka, one bottle of cognac, and fifteen beers. There were four of us, and with me limiting myself to beers and champagne, we managed to empty them all.

The Soviets never drank for taste. Mixing drinks for example was unheard of. So was sipping. Everything, including the wine, was consumed straight up in hard, fast shots.

The quantity imbibed on this night was average for such an occasion. As the evening progressed, Dimer called up some girls. There were four of us and three girls showed up—one for each of those guys. Even though I assured them I was okay, they were all apologetic that there wasn't a girl for me. They said sorry over and over and they meant it. Yes, yes they knew about Nicole, they assured me, but "you are guest in our country and must have Russian girl. Russian girls the best."

You had to be careful when declining an offer from a Soviet because, as was the case with Vika, they deemed it a personal insult. They felt that you were telling them that what they offered was not good enough. On more than one occasion Dimer walked away from me, saying, "We not happy you no like Russian girl."

They were so generous, and at the same time so vulnerable. I was at my buddy Rambo's place downtown and his mother gave me a bag of lemon pastries. They were good, roach-free lemon pastries and I knew enough, by then, not to leave them sitting on the top of a chair. But I made the mistake of not eating them the same night. A day later Rambo was in the room at the base and noticed there were still some lemon pastries around.

"Why you no eat mother's pastries?" he said with a wounded look. "You no like mother's pastries?"

I answered that I had already eaten several and that they were good. He wasn't pacified. The next night I was at his parent's place with all his family. Sure enough, Rambo brought up the business of the pastries. "Tod no like pastries. He no eat them."

I knew that no matter what I said in my defense, Mrs. Vasilenko would remain hurt.

10

Construction on the new athletic room at the base moved along at a standard socialist speed—a brick a day. Frequently I looked in on my way past to find the workers stretched out across the floor, having a smoke. Just another day at the office.

Easily three times as many employees as were necessary pretended to work at the base. As in the case of the kitchen's two-man soup team, the overabundance usually had the inverse effect—reduced efficiency.

The Soviet people of 1990 struck me as prepared to go to great lengths of generosity for anyone—so long as it wasn't in the name of the state. They would do nothing in the name of the state. They had long ago lost hope in their system. What remained was pride in themselves as individuals, and that's why they would open their doors and give what little they had and that's why they'd be so offended if I didn't eat all their pastries or indicate an appreciation of their women.

They were close to the soil, with good, basic values. Ramil Yuldashev was an example. If there was a star on the team it was Yuldashev. But he had no idea how to act the star. Permanently clad in a hopeless, powder-blue leisure suit, Ramil was unaffected, without airs, always prepared to go out of his way to make people happy.

We had two fans of the team who were semiretarded. They came to all the home games and to the road games they could get to by bus. They were hapless figures, but the players treated them kindly at all times, doing things such as inviting them on the team bus. Once, one of them came to Yuldashev with a stick he wanted signed. It was badly broken, but the fan was excited about having it anyway. He had gotten hold of it in the stands when a Soviet ref, as Soviet refs are wont to do, heaved it over the glass.

Yuldashev agreed to sign it, but the fan didn't have a pen. Half-dressed Yuldashev went around looking. He found one, but—no surprise for Soviet pens—it didn't write. By this time most players would have given up. Not Yuldashev. He looked again, finally found another that did work, signed the stick, and the retarded young man went away feeling like a million bucks.

The Soviets felt things deeply. I was at Rambo's apartment one day in the presence of his grandfather. A World War II veteran, Papa Vasilenko was among the Russian soldiers who joined a group of Americans in fighting against the Germans. Delighted to meet an American again, he spoke to me of that special moment in history, emphasizing how we are all part of the same human family, and how our two countries could work together like they did nearly half a century ago. A few minutes later the old man disappeared and brought back a suit jacket. It was covered in medals, and he put it on to show me. He stood erect in it, beaming proudly until tears began streaming from his eyes.

During the visit of my parents they asked a Soviet man who was well decorated if they could take his picture. Agreeing, he stood in a normal pose until my father pointed at one of the medals. Then he pulled his shoulders back, pushed out his chest, and stood as tall as possible, thrilled that we would take an interest in his achievements.

I'd see them and people like them and experience their generosity toward me and my parents, and then I'd see very different people—Soviets in their role as state employees.

During a team stopover in Leningrad I found a yellow canvas bag I wanted to purchase. A clerk was sitting on a stool, doing nothing, and I asked her if I could see it. She tried to ignore me, but since the other two clerks were actually busy, I kept asking. Finally acknowledging my presence, she gave me a surly look, and instead of simply turning around, lifting the bag from the shelf, and letting me look at it, she pointed to the other end of the counter and signaled me to go down there.

There, in this variation on the soup-serving routine, I found another clerk who was less ornery. She went back along the counter to where the first lady sat, showed me the bag, and I decided I would buy it.

Buying it meant going to a line to purchase a ticket

that in turn would allow me to join another line to get the bag. After ten minutes in the ticket line, I got my ticket and went to the other queue. But by the time I had moved up to the front of this one, all the canvas bags were gone. I got in another line, a refund line, to get a refund.

The whole process of not purchasing the yellow canvas bag consumed almost half an hour.

In the same city, one of the players wanted to buy his wife perfume but was unable. A new consumer edict declared that only Leningraders could purchase goods sold in Leningrad, only Muscovites could buy in Moscow, and so on, unless you were a foreigner and could pay in dollars like me.

On the way back to the hotel on a wet, very cold day we passed a store where there was a lineup on the sidewalk. The store was more than half empty and could have easily accommodated those waiting. But the policy of the state-run store was to allow only a few shoppers inside and let the others freeze. I asked Godyniuk why things had to be this way and he said, "Because it is socialism, this is why."

While I was in my room at the base writing in my log one night, Dmitri Khristich was there, hanging out. We were talking about something else, but Dimer interrupted. He pointed at my notepad and asked that I write something nice about the Soviets.

I looked over at him. "Country crazy, but people big hearts," he said.

He tapped his hand on the left side of his chest. "They good people."

Dimer and Sasha Godyniuk, each hoping to get permission to transfer to the NHL soon, would come to me and say, "Tell us about America." Then they'd sit and wait for me to talk about live entertainment, cars, sports, or anything American, not uttering another word themselves. They'd get huge smiles on their faces and a sparkle in their eyes.

I felt uneasy boasting about the U.S. all the time. I knew what I said carried great weight with them. We were all barely into our twenties and they were deciding if they would leave their families, their country, their entire way of life. They were great, gullible listeners. Like other young Soviets, they viewed the United States with an esteem that was almost scary. To them it really was heaven.

As we talked I was struggling to open a bottle of water. The fact that they didn't have twist-off caps was another example of how I missed the little conveniences of my normal life—flipping on a ball game, calling up a buddy, playing a round of golf, having freshly laundered clothes, eating a bowl of macaroni and cheese, mowing the grass, listening to the radio, reading the sports page.

This time Dimer came to my rescue with a small screwdriver that he carried around. He had about six different ways of opening non-twist-off bottle caps— screwdriver, his teeth, another bottle, a stick, a ring, the edge of a desk. I felt like a klutz every time—though I don't think Dimer and the rest of the guys expected me, an American, to have to take off my own bottle cap, just like they didn't expect me to wear Russian shoes. Americans were viewed as being a cut above, at least by young Soviets, and you would be treated as such so long as you accorded them respect and accepted their generosity.

Dimer and Sasha, having been drafted by NHL teams, were trying to obtain working visas so that the notion of defecting would not enter into the picture. Early on I used to joke with them about coming back on the plane to New York with me, but I stopped doing it because I knew how serious the whole thing had become.

Sasha Godyniuk had to wait until we went on a road trip to find an international phone to try to contact his agent in Vancouver. When I asked why he didn't do this in Kiev, he said, "Phone has ears in Kiev. People listen." The historic changes taking place in the Soviet Union, freedom of speech and other democratic initiatives, didn't excite the players or other Russians I met. They were committed cynics who simply could not believe their system could fundamentally change. They granted that some of Gorbachev's actions sounded promising, but figured in the end all would come to naught. Their Soviet fate in life was to hold up as best they could under tough, gloomy conditions. For a better life, they felt they would have to go elsewhere.

In our team bus we passed by a demonstration on the streets of Kiev. I was kind of dozing off, but the doc grabbed my arm, saying "Look, look!" The players moved to the side of the bus for a better view. But they were excited more by the novelty of the demonstration than by the prospect of real change. As the year wore on, they thought—wrongly it turned out—that Gorbachev was succumbing to pressures from the right wing and would reverse track on all the reforms he had brought in. During their one-thousand-year history the Russian

137

people had never experienced democracy, only dictatorship. Their cynicism therefore was hardly surprising.

In the town of Voskresensk I was cheered, however, to see some smiles on the streets. About seventy miles from Moscow, situated on the river, with many trees and wooded areas, Voskresensk reminded me of a small, handsome city in the United States. There was a peacefulness about it. I walked along a wooded path on the river's edge that brought me to the soccer fields that were so common to every Soviet population center. Soccer, or football as they called it, had reasserted its status as the number one sport in the Soviet Union after ice hockey had challenged and virtually caught up in the 1970s.

Beyond the fields on Voskresensk's two main streets, the stores were clean, reasonably well stocked, and the lineups small. I bought four crystal dishes, soap holders, and a toothbrush. Our hotel wasn't anything special but certainly outclassed the dungeon in Gorki. There were no bugs, the heating worked, and the beds were reasonably comfortable. On the down side, no elevator meant we had to climb five flights of stairs, there was no toilet seat or toilet paper or TV, you shared a washroom with the next room, and you had to walk outside in order to get to the dining room. There, though the food was standard Soviet fare, there was a unique feature—a different meal every time.

With a population of less than a hundred thousand, Voskresensk was a curiosity piece of the Soviet hockey league. While its percentage of the Soviet population was infinitesimal, it produced a wildly disproportionate number of great hockey players.

On the Soviet's 1988 gold medal Olympic team, four prominent players were natives of Voskresensk. They were Igor Larionov, Valery Kamensky, Alexander Chernykh, and Andrei Lomakin. Kamensky, who signed with the Quebec Nordiques in 1991, was a player who bordered on superstar status. Every time I saw him play I thought him capable of scoring four or five goals. He was coltish, with great loping strides that could take him effortlessly around defenses. His long reach would corral an escaping puck, and if he didn't want to be bothered deking the goaltender he could unleash a high bull's-eye wrist shot. But, as with many Soviet players, Kamensky's intensity would come and go like a summer's breeze.

Also among those from Voskresensk was Slava Kozlov, touted as the best junior player in Soviet hockey. Going back, it was Voskresensk that produced the three Ragulin brothers, most notably the famed Soviet defenseman Alexander "Rags" Ragulin, who patrolled the Soviet blue line like an oceanliner.

The town's team was called Khimik, after the local chemical factory that in the 1950s agreed to sponsor the club. Khimik reached the elite division in 1957, achieved a third place finish in 1965, and Voskresensk subsequently became a hockey-crazed town. Larionov recalled that "Everywhere kids were chasing a puck until they were dizzy. And everywhere the conversations were about last night's or tomorrow's match." In the Voskresensk summers they played hockey too. "When they sent us to a collective farm to harvest potatoes, we would grab a few potato sacks and make goal nets out of them," Larionov remembered. "We would sprinkle the pavement with sand to reduce friction and the game would begin."

Larionov was a young star on the Khimik team at the close of the 1970s, but under pressure from Tikhonov made the switch to Red Army. Virtually all the greats produced in Voskresensk were later lured to Moscow— another example of the feeder-system nature of the league. But even at the rate it lost its stars, the team was able to challenge the league's very best. It almost won the league championship in 1989, finishing second, and was near the top again the following year.

The town's arena, from the outside anyway, was one of the few on the Soviet circuit that fit the billing Palace of Sport. There were big fountains and neon lighting and good landscaping and no falling bricks. Inside, however, it wasn't much better than most other Soviet barns I played in. The Plexiglas was dirty and supported by thick metal frames that blocked the view of a large number of spectators. The scoreboard was antique and flanked by two ugly paintings of Khimik playing Canada. And like most of the rest of the Soviet Union, it needed a can of paint.

I often thought how the whole country would be so well served with the addition of a couple of very inexpensive items—paint and pancakes. The occasional pancakes you'd get for breakfast were terrific, but they came so rarely. Why they were looked upon as such a delicacy was hard to figure. I mean, how much does pancake batter cost?

The locker room attendant in Voskresensk, Jock, treated me like an old pal. He walked me back to the hotel, showed me around, helped me like Igor the hockey fanatic did in Moscow. Jock wanted to make a trade: my jacket, a red Eddie Bauer, for his—a brutal piece of sackcloth. I told him his was terrific but politely declined the offer. He made me promise to bring him an autographed stick the next time I came to town.

For the game, I didn't dress. I was all psyched to get out there, but at the afternoon meeting the coach announced my exclusion. Though my Russian was constantly improving, Bogdanov spoke too fast for me to pick him up and I had to turn to Dimer for a translation. Dimer gave me a sad look and said, "You no play." This got to be routine and I felt sorry for him having to do it all the time. He was embarrassed and so was I.

The advance publicity I had received in the cities we visited made the benchings all the more difficult. The fans were looking for the American. In Voskresensk a group of young teens found me in the stands and wouldn't let me go. They asked rapid-fire questions and followed me to a new seat each period.

Sitting in the stands at least afforded me a good view of some of the strange proceedings. In Leningrad our right winger, Oleg Sinkov, suffered a bad leg injury far from our bench. He tried to stand up and make it off the ice but couldn't. He was obviously in great pain, but though the referee noticed him, he let play continue. After trying futilely to push his way with his stick over to the boards, Sinkov dropped to the ice again, his face etched in pain. Now the linesman took action. But instead of blowing the whistle to stop play, the normal practice, he skated over to Sinkov, grabbed him by the shoulders, and pulled him to the bench like a sack of barley. All the while, play went on.

After the game I saw Oleg, still in pain, trying to hobble around on a crutch. The crutch was his hockey stick. I guess the medical supply staff wasn't up to scratch in Leningrad.

Rather than sit in the stands, I watched the Leningrad game from the bench. Without glass to separate us from the spectators, the fans kept up a running commentary with the players, liberally offering advice. Soviet fans were like that. They tended not to yell out stuff you hear in the States, like "You suck!" Instead they preferred rambling dissertations.

Near game's end, some fans were calling my name and I walked over. They asked me if I was Hartje and in a very friendly way threw a raft of other questions at me, the most frequent one being, "Why don't you play for Riga?" I guessed they were Latvians. I tried to explain why I was in Kiev but they kept saying "Go to Riga. Must go to Riga," as if I was really needed there.

Outside the rink, much later, I was met by a few kids who wanted autographs and by a Russian adult. He held an NHL players' guide opened to the page where my name was listed. He had stood outside in lousy weather for thirty minutes just to get me to sign the page. He was kind, and instead of just looking at each other warmly and getting the point across that our meeting was mutually pleasing, I wished we could have understood one another better.

But it's funny how a little kindness even from complete strangers can make a difference. Just when I was down, questioning my decision about being here, meeting him and the fans from Riga raised my spirits. They made me feel that something good from this curious venture would come.

11

My problems interpreting what the coach was saying fell to a new nadir at a team meeting in October. Bogdanov diagramed a play that, from what I could understand, we were supposed to carry out. I dutifully followed the instruction in a subsequent game. Afterward I discovered I had it wrong. What Bogdanov diagramed was a play we were *not* supposed to do.

I was learning several new Russian words a day, but one language faux pas followed another. At dinner at the base I wanted to compliment the new malnutritionist, Vera. She cooked with only an inch of grease in the pan—two less than the average of the other chefs. What I intended telling her was, "Gee thanks Vera, that was very tasty." Instead what I dumbly blurted was, "That was really sour Vera. Thanks a lot." The words for tasty and sour are quite similar in Russian. With any of the other cooks I wouldn't have minded mixing them up. But Vera was such a nice lady. Looking very sad at my pronouncement, she asked me if it was the milk or dessert that was sour. I apologized later when I was finally clued in.

My teammates got many a good howl from my linguistic performances. Boarding the plane to go to Riga, I tried to say to them, "This foggy weather makes me nervous about taking this flight." What came out was, "Because of this foggy weather, I'm pissing all over the place."

In situations unrelated to hockey, the mistakes weren't so important. But I never realized that language played such a prominent role on the ice until I tried playing the game in Russian. There are so many variables, so many strategies employed. You have to know not just the language, but the jargon, the sense, the tone. And of course with the speed of the game you have to pick the lingo up instantly. On my way up the ice with the puck, I'd hear an incomprehensible blur of Russian from the bench, from the stands, from my linemates. They were all telling me what to do next.

Compounding the confusion was the different game the Russians played, with its decidedly offensive orientation. Bogdanov did get around to explaining certain aspects to me in English, but it was impossible to cover them all. Once I was sent out on the penalty-killing unit. We played a box zone defense in such situations. I occasionally ventured from it in order to check the player at the point. When later I asked Bogdanov if what I was doing was correct, he said, "No, very wrong. You no go out to defenseman." He'd probably explained it earlier in Russian and I misunderstood. But I wondered, had I not approached him, how long he would have let me go on doing it.

Critical to making the line you play on successful is being able to anticipate what your linemates are going to do in certain circumstances. This can be worked out with time, but the process is made far more difficult when you can't come back to the bench and discuss what has just happened and arrange what to do in hypothetical situations.

I was quickly gaining an appreciation of the trials experienced by the first Russians who were playing in the NHL. A young kid like Alexander Mogilny joined the Buffalo Sabres knowing as little English as I did Russian. The great Vladimir Krutov, a cannonball forward who starred with Red Army for a decade, was struck by culture shock, language shock, and food shock (too many hot dogs) in Vancouver. A full-blooded, hammer and sickle Russian, he could not, despite his talent, make the switch. The Canucks soon dispatched him to the minors and he later left the organization to play in Switzerland.

I could look upon their miseries with some consolation. If world-class players had this kind of trouble making such an adjustment, no surprise that Tod Hartje wasn't lighting up the Soviet league.

We journeyed to a city of many beautiful onion-domed cathedrals called Yaroslavl. My line played the first period against Torpedo Yaroslavl (a slew of clubs were called Torpedo) and was benched for the second. Figuring I was done for the evening, I didn't pay much attention while Bogdanov diagramed a bunch of plays in the second intermission. Had I been paying attention

I probably wouldn't have understood anyway, but when he announced, as we stood up to go on the ice for the third, that he was looking to our line to get the job done, it was time for me to start guessing again. Our line did not get the job done.

Fortunately my dreams could take me away from it all. Back at the hotel, where my room was freezing, I put on a couple of sweaters and a parka, climbed under the covers, and fell into a sound slumber, one in which I dreamed I was eating my favorite flavor of ice cream— mint chocolate chip. It was so real that I woke up licking my lips, in the middle of the bowl. Then I dozed off again and finished it off. The longer I was away from home, the more I dreamed and the more vivid the dreams became. One had me at Michigan Law School with Nicole walking through the campus and going to classes. How I wished that one was true.

Sasha Savetsky, a talented forward on the team whom I called Sav, was dreaming of a girl from Ireland. He had met her while she was vacationing with friends in Leningrad a year earlier and was all excited now because he had received a letter from her. Sav, who in his brown leather jacket and blue baseball cap was one of the team's cool guys, couldn't read the English and gave the letter to me. I told him what it said, laying heavy emphasis on the best parts. This was great stuff for Sav and he asked me to write her back. I did, hoking it up with a lot of lovey-dovey stuff. "You're the girl of my dreams," the letter gushed. "I had heard of Irish eyes, but never knew their true beauty until I met you." On and on it went, enough clichés to challenge the Guinness record. I had been writing Nicole every single day, so the players knew I had a lot of practice at laying it on thick.

Problem was, there was no way the letter would have credibility in supersmooth English. So I explained to Sav what I'd written and had him repeat these thoughts in his terribly broken English with me writing them down that way. This made the letter appear authentic. Sav was so psyched about his first communication with a girl from the West that he kissed the envelope before putting it in the mail.

Unfortunately he never heard back. Either the letter didn't do the trick, or more likely, given the Russian postal system—pony express without the horses—it never got there.

Sav suggested one day that I should return to Kiev for another season and have my wedding here. When I told him that Nikki had two more years of law school and I couldn't do it, he suggested I tell her to quit and come on over. "Can't do it," I said. "She's the one who's going to be making the money for us."

It was a light, half-joking conversation, but the fact that Sav liked me enough to put forward such a proposal made me feel good. Given my problems with the hockey, it was the friendship with the Soviet players that kept me going. I was starting to enjoy my time away from the rink with them more than I was playing the sport.

The players were already exchanging addresses with me and getting me to pledge that I would write them and come back and visit. I did so in a paying-lip-service kind of way. Sav didn't like it. He grabbed me by the arm, looked me straight in the eye, and asked the ques-

tion again. I knew then that feelings were moving beyond the superficial.

After returning from Sav's one night the doc asked me
where I'd been. As I told him, he remarked that "Everybody on the team asks you to stay at their home. Who's
next?" A team official as well as some of the players
began calling me "Sokol boy." It was the ultimate sign
that I was being accepted and fitting in.

The team, like teams everywhere, had cliques and a
hierarchy. Players didn't get along with all the others.
But being new and so foreign I could move among them
all with a good degree of friendliness. I was their teacher
of the English language, I was letter writer, I was fashion adviser (hopeless task), I was consultant on the
United States, and in my latest task as the Westernizer
of the Sokol boys, I was dance teacher—for moves both
on and off the ice.

For the next party down the hall, it was a few different players who dragged me out of bed at one in the
morning. The highlight of the show this time was a new
girl, the comely and extroverted Vita. The many Soviet
girls I'd met fit primarily two types—outgoing, lively
party goers and quiet, antisocial grumps. Unlike the
men, the girls, both types, preferred a more formal look,
formal in the old-fashioned sense of the term. Their
styles were more akin to 1940s Hollywood than our time.

The comely Vita certainly fit the extroverted category
of Soviet woman. On this particular night she and one of
the other visiting girls got up to dance and really enjoyed putting on a show for the hockey players. Vita
wore a stretch miniskirt. It didn't stretch south as far as
taste might have required, and she weaved her body so

much it would have done a snake charmer proud. Responding, I pushed a chair out to the middle of the floor and, catching on right away, Vita was on top of it, continuing her act almost before it stopped sliding.

For music, the girls preferred Russian groups, but Bobby Brown was popular this night as he was generally around the base. I'm no Denny Terrio, but the dancing of Vita and her friends wouldn't have won any prizes. While there was a lot of movement, their style reminded me of junior-high stuff. There was no elegance in the coordination, and the effect was too lumbering. On request I gave them the latest floor moves I knew, and though they tried them, I think they found it all a bit strange—especially when I spun off on Brown's "My Prerogative" with the Chuckie Hughes style.

As for the latest in on-ice moves, I was a little hesitant to try to bring any razzmatazz to the Soviet game. Following my experience with the B team—trying to present the goalie with the puck and being looked at like I was from outer space—I'd noticed that high-fives, double pumps, or any of the typical NHL postgoal gyrations were not a part of the Soviet league. They didn't know how to celebrate goals with style. Taught not to show off, schooled in the laconic, the typical Soviet goal scorer maintained a studied damp-spiritedness. Many didn't even get their stick aloft. Some teammates, though never in a hurry to get there, would eventually make their way over to tap the scorer on the shoulder while the bench, unless it was a crucial goal, remained silent. Gradually I made progress trying to teach the Sokol boys the right moves, but it didn't seem to come naturally to them and I never scored enough myself to lead by example.

At a party, with a ton to drink and the music loud, the Russians could get boisterous and happy like any party goers. But they could rarely work up any high-powered emotion before, during, or after a game. To get pumped before going out on the ice, I played "Eye of the Tiger." That brought a lot of crazy stares from my teammates, whose way of getting psyched was to put a lot of sugar in their tea.

I wasn't sure if the emotion was repressed or if the nature of the system had sucked so many of the good juices out of the Sokol boys that there wasn't much life to begin with. But Fetisov's comment—that they'd been turned into hockey robots—seemed a telling observation. So many of the players had a defeatist edge. They didn't look to life as offering possibility. They seemed caught up in a grim routine, wholly resigned to a script already written.

Always they commented on my smile. None of them could believe I smiled so much. Though I was noted for having a ready smile back home, here it stood out like Vita on the chair. To Soviets, not just those on the team but everywhere, there had to be a major reason to smile. I tried to explain to the players that there didn't have to be a special reason. Why not smile anyway? What harm could it do?

"Easy for you," Vasilenko responded. "But life in Russia tough, always. No easy to smile." He told me about the gray life of his parents—their daily trek to work, their lining up for gas, food, and other products, their small apartment, their lack of time to do anything. For his mother it was most difficult because after working at the state job and doing the shopping, she had to spend the rest of the time in the kitchen—hence her dream of one day owning a microwave.

Vasilenko's parents hadn't gone out at night or been anywhere in years. Their spare time was spent in providing for the children. Vasily loved them. "Very good, my family. Parents give all to me and brother. Nothing for themselves." The Vasilenkos were so close, and indeed the Soviet families I met seemed closer knit than the American ones I had come to know. Hardship, the greater need to support one another, living together in such close quarters, created a tighter, if more despondent, bond.

The missing enthusiasm among the Sokol boys was deepened by the closed conditions in which they were made to live. We went on an eight-day road trip in October. Before it, when there were no games, the team was made to stay four straight nights at the base. All the isolation policy did was create resentment. "Life is baza, baza, baza," one of the team bachelors said. "I can't have normal life. Me single. For players with wife, it very, very bad."

I couldn't imagine being in a situation remotely close to this through my own years, say, eighteen to twenty-two. I was able in those days to do stupid things and live it up with my friends. I was able to grow and find out what I did or didn't want, and what I should stay away from. The regime they put the Sokol boys through left room for the occasional secret booze-up, but for no personal growth outside of hockey. And it was deliberate.

To create the masterpiece, as coach Igor Dmitriev said, you had to devote everything to the game.

Most of the guys were married and had young children they rarely spent time with. Most sad was when the families would come for a short visit after a practice or a game. After the games, the kids could accompany their fathers during the mandatory jog around the inside of the arena. Moments later, when they had to leave, the children would start bawling. They couldn't understand why their fathers couldn't come with them. The dads couldn't either. They would return to their little rooms at the base and do nothing the rest of the night except watch *Damien—Omen II* or Babar.

A couple of the Sokol boys went to the extreme of telling me they'd rather be in the United States in jail than in what they considered the equivalent of jail here. "I see in your movies," Vasilenko said, "that jail is better there. Football, baseball, relaxing, TV, telephone, cigarettes."

Others said being stuck at the base was like being in the army again, only this time the job was hockey instead of construction.

Apparent here again was the pervasive cynicism and negativism of the Russians. The idea behind the hockey system was that, like everyone else in Soviet society, you were paid by the state to do a job. Hockey wasn't supposed to be any more fun than construction work. And though you had to live in a camp, your occupation as a sportsman gave you several advantages other citizens did not have—better salaries, better food, more travel, more ready access to good cars and apartments.

Life wasn't supposed to be easy for anyone in the Soviet Union. Why should it be easy for hockey players?

It could have been easy. Though drinking would be a problem, the players likely could have played just as well, if not better, with relaxed conditions—with twice the amount of free time, with married players living with their wives and children, with a more positive mood struck by Bogdanov and the ubiquitous Teapot.

The Russian coaches seemed bent on keeping it joyless. Bogdanov dwelled on the negative. In the team meetings, the message invariably was that everybody was playing poorly. The players, as a consequence, often played without the abandon that would maximize their rich natural skills. Eyes were cocked over shoulders to the bench where the master presided. One mistake could mean being sidelined for an eternity.

Casting a further pall on the proceedings was the very grayness of the sporting milieu—the arenas, the fans, the dozing media. Though not as evident in bright Kiev as in the more dismal Soviet cities, the society, while changing under Gorbachev, was still shackled. The presence of state authority was still felt. As recently as the mid-1980s the state had in place a policy that forbade loud cheering in the central stadiums. Fans were permitted to clap, but anything more joyous would see them ushered out of arenas and ticketed by the militia. Foreign visitors to Soviet hockey games were shocked to hear between-period announcements over the public address system urging spectators to remain calm during the action so as not to violate the good socialist order. Many fans were only too happy to do so. One foreigner recalled a scene at a game in which two youths stood up to cheer their team during an exciting play and were roundly denounced by a patron sitting a couple of rows below.

An accident at a soccer game in Moscow in the early 1980s precipitated the clampdown. Many fans died at the end of the match when surging masses trampled over one another. The incident went unpublicized at the time, but strict crowd-control measures were put in place.

The sports media in the Soviet Union were, if anything, understated. The hype and superstar mania prevalent in the U.S. was almost entirely absent in Kiev. The newspapers ran short, boring game stories and shied away from highlighting personalities. Superstars sell sport, but if there were any in Soviet hockey the people of Kiev wouldn't have known much about them.

Glasnost, however, was now in place and some of the kowtowing of old was disappearing. Only a few years ago Soviet reporters had to submit each story to the athlete they were writing about to get his or her signature of approval before it could be printed. The athletes were, in effect, the editors. It didn't make for much of the other ingredient that sold sport—controversy. While this practice was diminishing, the sporting press was slower in picking up on glasnost than the political media. Virtually no advertising was allowed in the state media, another fact that only worked against the selling of the game.

While the Gorbachev revolution offered hope to some, its stripping away of the old communist belief system left Russians without an identity. Their traditional big celebration day of the year was November 7. This was Revolution Day, commemorating the advent of Lenin in

1917. But when November 7 arrived, it was dismally quiet. The Sokol boys recalled when they were little what a great celebration it was and how they were so proud and patriotic witnessing the fantastic parades of military hardware.

But now they realized the revolution had failed and that the day wasn't worth celebrating any more—though we did have a couple of shots. "Good day before," Savitsky said. "Now very bad revolution. No celebrate. But we drink anyway."

Soviet schools in 1987 had canceled their history exams, players told me, because glasnost had revealed that so much of what was in their textbooks was, to use an English word many of the players had picked up, "bullshit."

In the course of a conversation I mentioned I was going home for Christmas. The Sokol boys didn't know much about Christmas and I tried to fill them in. They did have a form of Santa Claus, a guy called Grandfather Frost who gave gifts to the kids around New Year's time.

What most of them wanted from Grandfather Frost this year was a one-way ticket to New York.

12

It was on our flight to the city of Minsk, the Belorussian capital near Poland, that the irony of ironies occurred.

To my Russian ensemble—the shoes, the passport, the drowsy bloodless look—I had recently added a Soviet topcoat. Like the footwear, it was the subject of widespread derision among the Sokol boys. To them, a dollar-spending American in a Soviet topcoat fairly boggled the mind.

It was getting so that sometimes I thought I looked as Soviet as they did—a conjecture that took on real life on the flight to Minsk.

Aeroflot was in fine form that day. The aircraft's vibration was so strong it shook my arms. The noise was so bad I might have been an inch from the engines. A metal bar inside the middle of the seatback rammed against my spine. It competed for penetration with the knees of the passenger behind me. The smell was a combination of rotten bananas and dirty socks. Limp warm water in an orange plastic cup unwashed since the invasion of Afghanistan was the sole refreshment.

I was in the first row, my foot propped up against the partition, wondering if we were going to fall from the sky, when the co-pilot happened by. He paused, looked over with half disgust at my suspended leg, and declared, "Who do you think you are—an American?"

As I tried to decide if I heard him right, the Sokol boys around me buckled over, barely able to contain their laughter. They confirmed what I suspected—thinking I was Russian, the co-pilot had given me a blast for acting like an American.

We thought about telling him who I really was, but let it go. I was carrying a Soviet passport, traveling under false pretenses to begin with. Blowing my cover might not have been a wise move. At any rate, when we deplaned I put on my best American smile and winked at him.

Some of my American habits, like the feet up or tossing stuff on the floor, were not appreciated here. The Sokol boys would gaze in astonishment as the floor of my room at the base became littered with shirts, socks, books, magazines. "In Russia we no put things on floor," they'd say. They kept their rooms and apartments neat. When you entered their apartments, putting on a pair of slippers was almost mandatory. Even with slippers, they didn't put their feet up.

We arrived at Minsk at twilight, but I could see a portion of the city and it looked almost as modern as Minneapolis. This, the guys told me, was about the best road stop on the Soviet hockey circuit. At our hotel, a long canopy adorned the entrance and big glass doors opened onto a lobby with leather sofas, lace curtains, and a swerving marble staircase. A lake in the center of the city with stands of tall trees along its banks fronted the attractive old portion of the city, or what the players called Little Switzerland. My hotel room, modern and heated, had a sink big enough to get my face in. Vasilenko and I were brushing our teeth when he saw my tube of Crest. "American, American," Rambo said. "I too have Crest from America. Very good, this very good."

In the lobby a guy came rushing over to us, shouting, "Bics for sale! Did you know? Bics for sale!" The news touched off a stampede. The Sokol boys swarmed the counter, buying six or seven packs of razors apiece, till all were gone.

With their clean shaves they went to the Panorama bar on the top floor and danced—with one another. I joined in, overcoming my initial reticence. In America, guys figure they're too cool to dance together. Here they go out and dance in a group often.

Our team had been doddling along, playing barely .500 hockey, but we won in Minsk 5–3. I played only the third period of what became, at least from the Soviet perspective, a violent game. Fights and rough play led to one of our players being ejected. He smashed an opponent over the head with his stick, then cross-checked him into the ice. The victim's teammates didn't bother rushing over to defend him.

The Russian game was still airy-fairy, Lady Byng stuff when compared to the level of violence in the NHL. One statistic told the story. Vladimir Kovin of Torpedo Gorki was considered the bad boy of Soviet hockey throughout most of the 1970s and 1980s. As the Soviets' all-time penalty leader, Kovin totaled 540 minutes in the box over twelve seasons. But for a big-time NHL pugilist, these numbers were laughable. Dave Shultz of the Philadelphia Flyers, for example, almost equaled Kovin's dozen-year output in a single season. He was penalized for 472 minutes.

But while still not approaching NHL standards, Soviet hockey was becoming increasingly rougher, moving away from its Bolshoi Ballet tradition to more gladiatorial combat. The Soviets claimed, probably with justification, that this was a result of the NHL influences. While increased exposure to the Soviet game had helped NHL players learn the pure art of the sport, Soviet hockey fathers moaned that the exchanges had actually hurt their hockey, making it dirtier, cheaper.

The violence in the Minsk game came shortly after I witnessed a hockey scene the likes of which I thought was confined to the West. I was watching a Soviet peewee match and was initially impressed by the display of skill and agility, especially from such pint-sized kids. But not far into it, though, the game turned into a dreadful show of goon hockey. Sticks to the head, slashes, vicious cross-checks. Two Russian kids, no bigger than bowling pins, started clubbing one another with their sticks. Another, more tame pair went at it with just the fists. The spectacle brought back to mind the Carlson boys in the film *Slap Shot*. Amazingly, no one was ejected or even stiffly reprimanded.

Soviet kids knew the NHL dream was reachable now and they also knew that the NHL demanded a tougher breed of Soviet hockey player. So they were prepared to play dirty. With the growing awareness that their own system was failing, the simplistic notion was widespread in the Soviet Union that anything American had to be good.

The reason why the Soviet Union topped the medal winners at most Olympics, summer and winter, was because of its sophisticated state-funded sports development program. Hundreds of specialized sports schools across the country began training kids at age eight. The system was still in place in 1990 and enough old guard Soviet coaches were around to foster its continuance. But the wholesale changes taking place in the country, including the pending move from state ownership to a free market economy, would likely mean an eventual abandonment of such a sports program. In the former East Germany, the sports-school system that produced a Katerina Witt and a fantastic Olympic medal harvest was already history, dismantled with the East German turn to the West.

At the state sports schools, the kids took a combination of regular academic lessons with athletic training every day. At age twelve a streamlining took place, the youths were channeled into their strongest sport for exclusive attention on it. This was accomplished with the aid of a muscle biopsy analysis in which a core of flesh was removed from the body to determine if the youngster had fast-twitch or slow-twitch muscle fiber. Slow-twitch meant they would be more suited to aerobic-oriented sports like swimming and cross-country skiing. Fast-twitch meant hockey, soccer, jumps, etc.

In the national network of sports schools, junior coaching was a full-time, fully paid occupation. A coach would take a group of promising hockey players at age

161

twelve and remain with them until eighteen, taking them through a stage-by-stage learning process. The coaches would then start again with a new group of twelve-year-olds.

In the United States and Canada there is no comparable system of schools with full-time hockey instructors. Development at the childhood and early teen level is ad hoc and not surprisingly tends to produce players with less subtle skills than the Russians. Exceptions are players like Wayne Gretzky, and one of the things that sets him apart is that he trained for the game in the imaginative way the Soviets did. When the Russians first played the Canadian pros in 1972 and everyone was gaga over the creative Russian approach, Gretzky, age eleven, wondered what all the fuss was about. "People said, 'Wow, this is really something incredible.' Not to me it wasn't. I'd been doing those drills since I was three years old."

The workouts for Soviet kids included ninety minutes a day on intricate dryland workouts and a battery of imaginative on-ice drills. They played scrimmages with thirty-pound belts tied to their waists, skated through obstacle courses, pulled along automobile tires tied to their waists, and did myriad jumps and kick exercises.

Brian Proctor, a prep school hockey coach in Ontario, took a group of Canadian teens to Minsk to work with Soviet youths for a few weeks every summer. He had wondered since he began watching the Russians how they came to have such impressive body control. After watching them at length he concluded that the pivots, the subtle shifts of weight, the extraordinary balance was more than God-given. In good measure it was taught.

"Can you imagine," Proctor asked, "the type of athletes we could produce in North America if we identified talent scientifically around the age of twelve and nurtured these teenagers through maturity at sports camps, making sure their diet, training, mental attitude, and competition were all finely tuned?"

In the Soviet elite division, the skills were supposed to be in place. To keep the body tuned to perform them, Bogdanov maintained heavy workouts throughout the regular season. On days when there was not a game scheduled we'd spend two hours in the morning on athletics (weights, running, soccer) and have one and a half hours of on-ice workouts in the evenings.

The training, I felt, was improving my skating, giving me more speed and acceleration. Being with them as well was giving me a better sense of how to use open ice space, and I was picking up odd things like knowing how to stop a puck when the other team tried to clear it around the boards. Rather than use the stick, the Russians would wedge their legs and butt against the boards, blocking it that way. It was much more effective.

But playing in a motivational vacuum wasn't easy. These players lacked an emotional edge to combine with their great skills. It seemed nothing could shake these guys. They would play a game the same way no matter if we were winning or were losing. Against the Moscow teams we would take a lead, and instead of getting psyched to hold it, we'd play at a laconic tempo and watch it drift away.

The Sokol boys didn't get angry. They would never come off the ice swearing at the opponent the way players did in the leagues where I came from. But if someone on our team miscued, they'd yell at him and curse him at the bench.

They'd rarely take on the refs. After bad penalty calls, instead of calling the refs every dirty Russian name imaginable, our guys would give them a disappointed, puzzled look and skate off.

The Sokol boys were overly impressed by the order of things. They respected, sometimes revered, another team's ability to the point that when a Moscow team came to town they thought it only right that the Moscow team win. Their prophecy was usually self-fulfilling, and because it was the order of things they didn't feel bad about it. We didn't have a resident tough guy to stir up emotion, jerk us out of our normal, forever rhythm.

This was evident when we played Spartak. Formed from an amalgamation of small trade unions in the 1930s, it was by tradition the Soviet people's team, the team the little guy rooted for. The Spartakians, probably as a result, were a more spirited bunch. They had a big defenseman who would crunch opponents into the boards, and once when he flattened one of our guys with a furious hit it looked as if the Sokol boys would get angry. They came to the dressing room swearing that they'd get him in the next period. But in the next period nothing happened. They said next game. But in the next game, nothing happened.

No matter how much Bogdanov kept emphasizing the need for "harakter, harakter," character was a tough commodity to find on a Kiev team that was always quick to despair.

Many incentives were built into the system to put stakes in the game and make them play harder. The more you scored, the earlier you got a car. The better you did, the earlier you got an apartment. The more your team won, the more bonus money you won.

As a base salary I was paid between 300 and 350 rubles a month, a little higher than the team average. The team average in turn was higher than that of the average Soviet worker, who got less than 200 rubles a month. Augmenting the base salary were bonuses for scoring points, finishing high in the standings, winning individual games. In addition there was that big plus for winning a home game. It usually meant a free night away from the base.

Some of the players already had cars and apartments, so that those particular incentives no longer applied. Money as an incentive didn't work in a lot of cases because veterans already had wads of rubles, and besides, there was nothing to buy in the stores anyway.

Coupled with the incentive program to shake the Sokol boys from their stupor was the required discipline. But the flippant attitude toward ruble money made the fines imposed by management for bad behavior something of a joke. To be caught smoking, for example, was a twenty-five-ruble fine. But virtually everyone on the team smoked as soon as the coaches were out of sight. Bogdanov or Teapot would frequently appear in the dressing room, so the players wouldn't smoke there. But it was a simple matter of moving to the showers in the room behind. There, they lit up before and after the cold water poured. If they got caught, so what? Twenty-five rubles? Pfff.

The Sokol boys smoked filterless Russian cigarettes that gave off a thick strong smoke that clung like glue. When they dragged on them, tobacco from the nonfilters would fall into their mouths and they would spit it out. When a bunch of them were together doing this it took on a Monty Python look and became hilarious to watch. Take a drag, have a spit. Take a drag, have a spit. That was the routine.

For successive alcohol violations, fines were 150, 200, and 250 rubles, with the added threat that you could be kicked off the team. But the unwritten rule was that if you were a good player, management wouldn't take drastic measures. Defenseman Sergei Lubnin got caught boozing four times. He was a good player. Nothing happened.

Lubnin was somewhat of a dinosaur, an old-fashioned communist who viewed Stalin as the greatest of Soviet leaders. One of the team's leading power-drinkers, he was big on the three necessities of Soviet life—potatoes, vodka, and cigarettes. He had them in equal proportion.

As my Christmas break neared, an air of unease swept the camp. Economic conditions in the city deteriorated to the extent that everyone on the team was given a bag of food products—fruit, sausage, and a can of some other unidentifiable meat. Political and economic chaos and confusion gripped the country. No one was quite sure whether perestroika and glasnost would succeed or whether there would be a reversion to the old system. Whatever the shakedown, the team was feeling the thunder. There were rumors that we were going over to private ownership—any day now. Joining the exodus of Soviet skaters abroad, two of our leading players, Yuldashev and Sherayev, signed to play in Finland for next season. They were both veterans, and for veterans whose peak abilities had passed, it was easier to get permission from the hockey establishment to leave. It was said that Bogdanov, who had logged a dozen years with Sokol Kiev, would follow suit to a coaching assignment in Scandinavia. And no one knew how much longer the two fun guys on the team, Khristich and Godyniuk, would be with us.

Godyniuk was getting ready to bolt. The Leafs weren't prepared to buy out his Sokol contract and Sokol wasn't prepared to let him leave freely to join the Leafs. He told me he had no choice. It was either Soviet hell or North American heaven.

The more patriotic Khristich didn't see it in such simple terms. The motherland was strong in him. He was tense, wanting to go and yet not wanting to go. What would he do in Washington, all alone, by his "one self" as he put it. "You be home next year," he said to me. "But I go for life."

Unlike Godyniuk, Dimer wanted the Sokol team to get a big chunk of the money from any deal made with Washington. It would be his way of saying thanks to the Soviet system. It had developed his hockey talent, he felt. It had given him everything he had. Defecting was out of the question. The bridges had to remain in place.

In Finland, on the exhibition tour with the team in the summer, Dimer had met a sports agent. The agent hung out with him and they were friends and so, Dimer said,

"I sign contract." The contract gave the agent a very high 25 percent on profits from endorsements and investments. Dimer had me look it over, and I had to tell him that I didn't think too much of it. "Yeah well, I no speak language," he said. "How can I know dis contract?"

It was easy to sympathize with him. How could he know what agents make, where he should put his money, what to demand from the Washington team. I called an official of the Caps to alert them to the situation and Dimer felt better. The advice from Washington was to tell him to lie low and not upset Bogdanov. The Capitals and Kiev had yet to reach a final agreement on a deal for Sokol surrendering the star player.

Growing up as hockey stars in their closed Soviet world, the Sokol boys were like players in an earlier American sports era in that they were wowed by the prospect of the big time. Blinded by the light, they were prepared to sign almost anything. They had no legal representation, no players' union. The sports bosses controlled the show and the players got a pittance.

So it was with Dimer. As a seventeen-year-old, Khristich had had a one-on-one meeting with Bogdanov, and signed a single piece of paper that, though he didn't know it, legally bound him to Bogdanov for about as long as the coach wanted. So now he was dependent on the goodwill of the coach. Fortunately for him the coach was preparing to leave as well—though Khristich didn't know this at the time.

I was trying to learn hockey and the language but had become caught up in the controversies of Dimer and Sash, who came to me for advice, and in the lives of the other players and families who kept inviting me to their apartments. Once they've taken you in, opened their doors to you, Russians expect loyalty. To say no is to offend them—no matter how sensible your rationale may be.

Savetsky's kind parents saw me after one game. I had said a few nights earlier that maybe I would go to their place. But I ended up begging off because I was tired and had a phone call booked to Nikki at eleven o'clock.

The Savetskys were deeply hurt. "Why didn't you come to our home?" the father asked me that night after the game. "My wife thinks it's because you did not like your last visit." I explained about the phone call I had booked. "You could have come after your phone call," he said.

I had only just been in hot water for not eating all of Mrs. Vasilenko's lemon pastries. I had offended a team-mate for not meeting him downtown with two girls he had lined up. Vika was angry because I hadn't followed up on something with her. And I was still trying to get back on good footing with Vera the cook after thanking her for her sour food.

To the Savetskys I apologized several times, where-upon they insisted I come over that night—even though it was after ten and there was school for their kids the next morning and practice for us. I couldn't say no. It was impossible to explain, even if I could have done so in English, that I needed some privacy, that I had already been to their house several times, that I hadn't had a night to myself in so long, that I just didn't feel like going again—even though I thought they were great.

Neither the Savetskys nor their daughter drank. Good for them, but for me it meant a more difficult evening. It was much easier to spend these nights half in the jar than cold sober. With the vodka flowing and everybody wrecked, I wasn't so embarrassed about my Russian, the conversation flowed more easily, and the time went faster.

I went over that night and it was tea and cake and compote and sandwiches and apples and more tea and cake and sandwiches and compote and apples. Mrs. Savetsky emptied the fridge, as she usually did. I enjoyed myself but felt so much pressure in trying to convince her of this fact that I was uneasy. The next day Mr. Savetsky saw me at the arena and introduced me to a friend of his as "my son Tod."

The Savetskys had a daughter whom I disappointed to the point of tears one night because I didn't make it over. She was part of a dance troupe, and for the big show she had purchased a new costume. She wanted me to see her in it before she left town for the performance. She waited for me till she was late. I couldn't make it. Tragedy.

In late November I met with Bogdanov. I was hoping to get approval for my plan to return home after our last league game on December 4 and come back at the end of the month. But they hadn't bothered to inform me about the December schedule, and when Bogdanov began telling me about exhibitions in Czechoslovakia and Germany as if I would have to be there, I began to worry. It sounded like all I was going to get off was about a week. "You need these games to stay in condition," he said. But I had a counter to this argument. I had been invited to play for Team U.S.A. in a Christmas tournament. This, I told him, would keep me in the best of shape. Bogdanov thought about it for a couple of minutes and said, "Okay, you go December 4."

I rushed off a letter to Nikki in which I told her the good news and other tidings.

13

R ambo and I were walking in downtown Kiev, cut into an alley behind stores, and caught sight of workers unloading a meat truck. The men were putting unwrapped slabs of meat on cardboard spread across the ground. They were careless and there wasn't much cardboard. Lots of the meat sat on dirt.

Not long after, I climbed into the back of one of the team minibuses, used to transport equipment and food. A strong smell from the gasoline cans piled in the van didn't bother me as much as the sight of camp food supplies strewn under sticks, pads, and other equipment. Unwrapped loaves of bread lay there with as many flies buzzing about them as had been attacking the meat unloaded from the truck.

With food quantities in short supply across the country, I was hearing more and more horror stories about restaurants. Waiters were scraping the used food from plates onto new ones for the next customers. The same with drinks—unfinished milk or Pepsis poured into a new glass until it was full.

I used to frown at Harvard's postgame box lunches. Tuna, ham, turkey sandwiches on white bread with mustard and mayo. Oranges, potato chips, a folded napkin. I'd throw that lunch away half the time and buy another. "Well, son," Mom wrote me, "those Harvard lunches don't look so bad now, do they?"

At the end of November we left on our final road trip before the Christmas break to the metropolis of Chelyabinsk, a city near the Ural mountains that had a team called Traktor. Sergei Makarov, the Russian who joined the NHL's Calgary Flames in 1988 and became the league's rookie of the year, began his career with Traktor Chelyabinsk. The city was known for Makarov and, as the doc told me, one other fact of note: Chelyabinsk was the motherland of the Soviet hydrogen bomb. In the 1950s when Americans thought they were far in front in the arms race, the Soviets unveiled their hydrogen bomb, then sent *Sputnik* into orbit, then in 1961 put the first human, Yuri Gagarin, into outer space.

It was a different sports era then, one when Soviet hockey players were true believers, true patriots, willing to sacrifice everything to win for the motherland. Gagarin himself was a hockey fan who later founded a team in Star City, a Soviet space research center in the tall pines near Moscow. Vitaly Davidov, an outstanding defenseman of the time, remembered that when the news flashed that Gagarin had successfully completed his first space flight, his teammates were in the dressing room preparing for practice. They went out with their

173

spirits so high, he said, that they literally flew across the ice the entire day.

Now the only place Soviet players wanted to fly was out of the country. The day we left for Chelyabinsk, Godyniuk made his move. He informed the club he couldn't make the trip because of a leg injury. How serious the injury was, or if there even was one, I'm not sure. But Dimer and I knew that when we got on the plane for Chelyabinsk we had seen the last of him in Kiev.

He told the two of us that while the team was away, he'd be leaving through Yugoslavia with his girlfriend and his agent for Toronto. Godyniuk had concluded that the team wasn't prepared to let him go for another three or four years, but he wasn't prepared to wait that long. The Leafs wanted him, but not enough to pay the huge sum that would be required to have Kiev release him.

Because Godyniuk's plans had to be hidden, Dimer and I couldn't give him a rousing send-off. It was obvious Sash hadn't slept in a few days. His mood seemed more excited than scared or unhappy. His parents knew and were supportive. His girlfriend, a Soviet model, was more reluctant. By Soviet standards they both had it so good, and I think they knew that. But Sash wanted it better. I grabbed his hands, wished him well, said I'd see him in the big leagues, and got ready for the next Sokol road trip horror show.

A no-drink, no-food three-hour flight got us to Sverdlovsk, which was a four-hour bus trip from Chelyabinsk. Five or six of us needed a bathroom but there was none in the building where we claimed our luggage. This meant a trip to the main terminal. But a thorough search

of the main terminal turned up no bathroom there either. Shaking my head in disbelief, I trekked across the
tarmac in subzero temperatures with the other freezing
Sokol boys till we found an area of seclusion.

No restaurants were open in the Sverdlovsk airport.
We boarded a bus for the long trip to Chelyabinsk, and
as was normal for Soviet buses, it broke down. When we
reached the hotel, breakfast was not being served there.
Because of unknown complications, our rooms weren't
ready and we waited three hours in a cold lobby with
few chairs. On my assigned floor the "duty lady" with
the key wasn't around so we had to wait another fifteen
minutes there. The room was even colder than the one in
Yaroslavl where I wore my parka to bed. The water was
dirty and stank like a swamp. I couldn't wash in it.

My ceiling was leaking badly, and when doc came by
I asked him about it. "It happens often," he said, dis-
missing the complaint. "It is all part of your Soviet education."

At the rink I was interviewed by two journalists from
the local newspaper. Both had pens that didn't work.
They wrote about my big white-toothed smile. All Soviet papers wrote about the novelty I brought to the
Soviet Union—my big smile.

Back at the hotel, I spent several minutes on the elevator trying to get to my floor. The elevator had buttons
to press but no numbers to go with the buttons and no
arrows to indicate whether you were going up or down.
People were rushing on and off, like the Keystone Kops,
trying to find out what floor they were on. All part of my
Soviet education.

Dinner was like something you would feed your most

desperate pet animal. The meat (I heard they served horse meat around here) sat in some god-awful juice looking like Alpo. One staple you could always count on in the Soviet Union was potatoes. But here there were no potatoes. I went back to my room, hungry, cold, and tired.

I was able to book a call to Nikki at 4 A.M. We spoke for twenty-three minutes at a cost of 138 rubles. The women working at the hotel were astonished. I'd spent the equivalent of almost a month's pay for a Soviet worker on one phone call.

Home from Chelyabinsk with a stop in Moscow for a loss to the Soviet Wings, the team discovered that there was no Alexander Godyniuk. Bogdanov called Godyniuk's mother. She told him Sasha went to bed one night and the next morning was gone. Bogdanov broke the news to the team before a practice. Observing my attempt to keep a straight face, Dimer put his head down and did all he could to keep from laughing.

Everyone knew that Godyniuk and I hung around together some, and with me being American, I'm sure there was suspicion that I was privy to the plot. A few guys made jokes that with Godyniuk having gone West I would now be forced to stay East to even things up. But no one said anything accusatory. Many got a kick out of Mrs. Godyniuk's story, including Bogdanov. But the coach was annoyed because the team could well have used the dollars they might have received in a deal for the player. "No Sasha. No money," Bogdanov said.

Only a couple of days after the news Dimer came walking, or I should say floating, into my room after a session with the coach. I knew by the look on his face that this was it, that he was gone too. From two earlier meetings with Bogdanov he had emerged almost in tears. Bogdanov had told him he would have to wait and Dimer, afraid to challenge the coach, wouldn't push the matter. Now the player told me that the deal had been struck—the Capitals had reached an agreement with Sokol on his leaving. He would be going to Washington in a few days to start play immediately.

Kiev had lost two of its best players, and two of its best party guys. I had lost the buddy who sat on my right in the dressing room and the one who sat on my left. I was happy for them both but disappointed from a selfish point of view. In a short period of time, we, Dimer and I in particular, had become close.

Their departure probably was the factor behind my funk of the next few days. I wanted to leave but couldn't. I couldn't write letters because I knew I would be home before the mail arrived anyway. I began packing a week early. I kept going over in my head what I had to do before taking off. Time was standing still and I had this bad feeling that after returning home for Christmas I would have to come back. No matter how much I had grown to admire these people, I wanted to go home for good now. I was learning about myself. "Guess I'm just a momma's boy," I wrote in my log. But then I thought—how many momma's boys would have done this in the first place? How many would have left such comfortable home situations, girlfriends they loved, to isolate themselves like this for so long?

At any rate I was soon out of funk city. The arrival of Mike Smith, the Winnipeg manager, gave me a lift. He was "the man" from the organization, someone to reconnect me with my real world, someone to remind me that I hadn't just been shipped to the USSR and forgotten about.

"The people love you here," he told me. "You've made a great impression." Hearing it made me feel good. Only the day before I had given a little girl one of my sticks after warm-ups and saw the joy in her eyes as she went running across the lobby to her mom to show her. I had just received a letter from a girl in the southern Armenian republic. She had read an interview in a newspaper with me. She was simply writing to welcome me to her country.

I would have these black periods, particularly because of my uncertain progress with the hockey team. But I was always picked up by the big Soviet hearts. After the next game we played, I stepped outside the dressing room to be greeted by Vika. As we talked, the Savetskys came over, then the Yuldashevs, then the Vasilenkos. Other kids, other adults would come up, say hello, have me sign something. Then there were those who insisted on giving me things—sandwiches, pastries, cookies, gifts to take home for my parents. It was hard to believe how giving these people were. Sometimes I wished all of the United States and all of the other people in the world who had misjudged them had been there to see how they treated me.

In the last days before leaving I spent a lot of time with the Yuldashevs, Ramil and talkative Toma. Ramil was a cheery guy who didn't get the recognition he deserved for his scoring exploits, yet he didn't let it bother him. Toma, the one who took my parents to the opera, was a notch above all the other Soviet women I met. Unlike so many Soviets, she hadn't let communism dim her spirit.

Though they had more than most Russians, the Yul-dashevs didn't have a lot. They still, for example, had to wash dishes in between the courses of the dinners in order to have enough. Their most exciting news in a long time was the pending arrival of new furniture—a sofa, a dresser, two chairs, and two footstools.

Toma was so excited that for arrival day she had her hair done, put on a new dress, and being a lover of perfume, wore scads of the stuff. When the doorbell rang, she danced around the apartment wearing a grin so fantastic I thought her face was going to burst. For the delivery man she got out cake and wine and played music and we had a furniture arrival party. We rearranged the room various ways and Toma must of have sat on each new piece a hundred times. I got pumped just watching her.

Toma was happy in the Soviet Union. I thought Vika was that way too—until she approached Mike Smith for a job in Winnipeg. She had told me in August that though she thought highly of the United States, she would never leave the Soviet Union. I believed her then and continued to believe her. Smith couldn't help her, of course, and I asked her why the change of mind. She didn't respond. I asked a second time and again got nothing. She would only say, "The answer is not short. I will tell you when you come back."

I left by train for Moscow, where I would then get a flight to Helsinki and on to New York. I had four major-size luggage pieces and several small ones, but didn't have to handle them myself because so many others were there to help. Vika accompanied me in the minibus to the station after the players had loaded it up. Of course, Igor the hockey fanatic was the first to meet me getting off at the station and rushed around helping in the only fanatical way that he knew how. The players had arrived to help me get the stuff on the train too, and after that was done I stepped out to say goodbye.

By this time it seemed that almost everyone I knew in Kiev had arrived, and I began to get intense and choked up as I moved to embrace them. When you're accepted as part of the Soviet family I suppose you should expect this. I'd seen how, when anyone was leaving the city for even the most routine of excursions, the families and relatives would appear at the station and the hugging and kissing and flower-giving and well-wishing would begin. The bonding was so thick.

But I wasn't prepared for that day at the station. Those families didn't have to come. It was like I was leaving for an eternity. They were so warm. They said goodbye, safe trip, best to your parents, we will miss you, and naturally they handed me gifts.

The kids, the small Soviet children who treated their elders with such respect, came forward and shook my hand. They learned to shake hands early. Among Soviet men, shaking was as common a gesture as saying hello. Even if you'd seen a guy only a few hours earlier, you'd often shake his hand the next time you saw him.

As the train pulled out and I made eye contact and the Soviet families waved and blew kisses, I felt like I'd been adopted by them. Suddenly that thought of coming back after Christmas didn't feel so terrible any more.

To top the splendid send-off I was met in Moscow by a baggage man who recognized me as the American hockey player in the Soviet Union. He was thrilled and did all he could to help me. I was skippingly happy, but the highlights, unfortunately, ended there.

Everything, I thought, had been arranged. I had a ticket that was supposed to be waiting for me at the airport. I had a visa that was supposedly valid for another half a year.

But when I arrived at the airport only thirty minutes before the scheduled takeoff due to a mix-up with my soldier driver, I discovered that my tickets were back at the Finnair reservation desk in the center of the city. I had no time to get back downtown, get the tickets, and make the flight. It left without me.

I didn't know how to react. I was angry at myself, Winnipeg, Sokol, the airport, the airline, the embassy, God, life, country.

No other flights from Moscow could get me to Helsinki in time for my scheduled plane to New York. With my ton of luggage I headed back into town to the Hotel Sport where athletes have preference. Some military punk was driving me. I had been angry at him on the way to the airport because he kept demanding goods from me. Now before taking me back downtown he was insisting on a big dollar price—too dumb obviously to realize that I was in the blackest of moods imaginable. I gave him twenty-five rubles and told him to get moving. He went only a few miles, stopped the car, and said that was it. Had I a touch more of a violent strain in me, I swear I would have banged his head against the trunk until he was cold dead.

I was able, finally, to get a cab to the hotel. Still in a state of rage, I was relieved to find that two of my Harvard buds, Tim Perry and Mark Bianchi, who had been visiting Moscow, were still here at this hotel. I left my bags with a note for them and hitched a ride on a tourist bus filled with Canadians to somewhere not far from the Finnair office. It was closing, but I got there in time to discover that the next day's flight to New York from Helsinki was canceled. I would have to wait a couple of more days.

I got back to the Hotel Sport where Tim and Mark were in their room with my bags. They started laughing when they saw me. "You're such a screw-up, Hartje. You always were."

They took me to the hotel restaurant where we got their favorite waiter—the Eel. The called him the Eel because he was always trying to slime his way into a deal with them. He worked a barter system. He'd bring out more food depending on what you had to offer— cigarettes, dollars, pens, hockey sticks. As I told the guys, their Eel was just one in a million.

For my next attempted departure, I got to the airport two and a half hours before takeoff. I got through customs and baggage check easily enough, but the last guy, the visa check man in a lighted booth, stared at my papers for the longest time and finally, raising his head, declared, "Big problem."

He explained that my visa had expired, that I wasn't even supposed to be in the country. I tried paying him fifty-five dollars for an application to extend it, but was told the process usually took days.

Ready to climb through the roof, I explained in Russian to the guards that I played for Sokol. Fortunately they were hockey fans and picked up on who I was.

Knowing this, and seeing my look of desperation, they made quick work of renewing my visa after calling down their boss.

After my three days of trying, I boarded the plane for an all-American takeoff. During my Moscow holdover, the Mrs. America pageant was being held in the city in conjunction with the Miss USSR one. On boarding the aircraft I was met by the sight of dozens of superattractive women. At first I didn't catch on, but then I got talking to an American. Turned out he was the trainer for Mrs. New York, the first runner-up.

When the plane got airborne, the gals began singing *America the Beautiful.* On the way back I listened to them bitch all the way about the conditions, the food, the hotels, the cockroaches. I'd heard it all. I'd seen it all. And I didn't need the replay.

14

On board Finnair, heading back to the Soviet Union, Christmas break over, a thousand thoughts were going through my head, most of them good: "I know what to expect this time. I have friends there, I'm comfortable among them. I understand why I'm doing it now. I can see the benefits. Nikki will be coming over to visit me in a month."

As Dave Letterman said—yeah, there I was on the Dave Letterman show, still can't believe it—it's no Club Med. But he doesn't know the people.

The media interest back home overwhelmed me. All the heavyweights—the talk shows, the New York *Times*, *USA Today*, CBS Sports, interviews, interviews, interviews. Instead of a broken down team bus, limousines. Instead of soggy oat balls, Manhattan's finest restaurants.

When I'd left the U.S. in June, I never thought I'd find

myself defending the Soviets. I didn't try to minimize the problems the country faces. There are as many as I ever imagined. But when you can understand a situation and the people in it, you can feel much more sympathetic.

My first meal back in the United States was hot dogs with a ton of mustard. Never tasted so good. With Nikki, my first stop was Bob's Pizza. Never tasted so good.

Nikki was in the middle of law exams when I got back. She'd been in the airport in New York for about eight hours, up behind a pillar on the second floor, trying to study contracts. Seeing her wasn't what I expected. We both stood there, dead tired, numb, looking like you do in airports, not knowing what to do or say.

She couldn't believe my appearance—so pale and skinny compared to when I left. I got the same reaction from everyone. "What happened to you?" "God you look awful." "Don't you eat anymore?"

What an eye-opener it was over the holidays to see how spoiled Americans are. I played hockey with a minor league team to stay in shape. On our one long bus trip to Peoria, Ill., we had all the comforts—big comfortable seats, juicy steaks, music, beers, snacks, modern hotels, VCRs, heat, hot water, pastries without the cockroaches. To the Russians it would have been heaven. To me, veteran now of Gorki, of Chelyabinsk, it was heaven. To the Americans it was the opposite. "How much further?" "This is brutal." "I'm dying." "Get me outta here."

Hearing the abuse, I could only smile. Russia had already taught me one of life's vital lessons—keeping things in perspective, being thankful for what you have.

Though I'd come to admire the Soviets, climbing back

into a U.S. uniform with twenty of my fellow Americans was sheer delight. The camaraderie, the understanding, the common culture, common language, knowing the systems, MTV, being able to talk on a phone and call Nikki after a game, not being afraid to use the bathrooms for fear of rare diseases, etc., etc.

The Soviet team represented in the Christmas tournament was Dynamo Riga. When I saw them, I shuddered. The reality—I play for one of those teams—kicked in abruptly and hit further as I watched them. Having spent some time defending the Russians I was dismayed, thoroughly embarrassed by the boorishness of this particular team. Their hockey was superior—they won the tournament. But they responded to the taunting of the crowd with atypical comportment—spitting at refs, throwing tantrums, stealing our habit of showboating after goals, and, I hesitate to say, evincing a level of hygiene best left for septic tanks.

In Albany, N.Y., a bunch of my teammates got off the same elevator as the Riga players and came flying into my room like they were escaping mustard gas. "What a reek! Holy shit! Don't they ever shower? How can you stand it over there? Take them back some deodorant for Christmas, will ya?"

From experience I knew they took showers after the games and did their laundry as often as I did. But their equipment was much older, and soaked in sweat as often as it was, it could give off an obnoxious smell. Occasionally during games I'd catch this odor on the bench and gag. I'd get up, pretend that I was fixing my equipment or that I needed a new stick, and move to a different seat. Another source of the aroma problem was probably the Soviet penchant for wearing the same clothes a lot. They'd go on an entire eight-day road trip with one shirt, one pair of slacks, one sweater.

It became a losing battle trying to defend the Riga team—their nerd haircuts didn't make it big either. Nonetheless, the Christmas hiatus was what I needed, and as the plane landed at Moscow's Vnukuvo Airport I was a confident young man.

By coincidence on TV in the lobby the Red Army team was playing my Western team—the Winnipeg Jets. It was one of the games in the annual superseries, a series that the Soviets won again.

The bartering began with the taxi drivers for the trip downtown. Many vied for a combination payment from me—ten dollars American plus twenty rubles, or thereabouts. But I was a veteran of these wars now, sized up the field, pulled a hockey stick from my sheath, and held it forward. With that, they were practically on their knees. The deal was struck. The trip to town, one hour, for one stick.

On the connecting flight to Kiev a man named Said from Uzbekistan, a Soviet republic down near Afghanistan where I thought they never heard of the sport, peppered me with questions on hockey in the USSR versus hockey in the U.S.A. Many Soviet people considered me a famous citizen, he said, and were referring to me as the "Little Sparrow."

Little Sparrow? He explained that there is an old Russian adage having something to do with the notion that the first birds back after a long cold winter are the sparrows. After decades of a freeze in American-Soviet relations, Said noted, I was one of the first Americans to

187

come back and take up a role in Soviet society. "For American to play in our hockey league, such crazy idea before," he said. "Now you here. Things change for better with our countries."

At the base I was greeted with bear hugs. The Sokol boys were surprised to see me. They thought that once back home I would stay there. Our first workout, two hours of running and lifting without any water, had me wondering myself, as did the first meal—soggy oat balls.

Nothing had changed—except five of the Sokol boys had new cars. They'd bought them on their exhibition swing through the former East Germany. Waiting in the USSR was too long a prospect, so Germany became the solution.

Poor Yuldashev—I really felt bad for him. What happens in this country, it seems to me, is that a lot of people drive without learning. To get a driver's permit doesn't require much of a test. I'd been in cars with a few of the young Sokol boys before and their carefree approach was evident. No need for a breaking-in session in a parking lot or back alley. Not having driven before, they just went out there on the big boulevards and let loose.

Yuldashev, who had waited so long and so longingly for his own car, had hardly done any driving. On his way back from Germany, with only a handful of kilometers on the car, he got in his first crash. The car survived that one in one piece. Second day back at the base though, Yuldashev went out for another spin and the car never came back. He totaled it. Ran headlong into a stanchion. The car was a write-off, and there was no such thing as Soviet auto insurance to pay for a new one. Yuldashev was devastated. He looked as wrecked as the car did.

Several of the guys got caught drinking on the Czechoslovakian leg of their Christmas tour. Five of them were fined, one for the third or fourth time this season, and they kicked Valery Butvenko off the team. He was a borderline leftwinger to begin with and the boozing gave the coach an excuse to dump him.

With Dimer and Godyniuk gone, the drinking and partying at the baza slowed. While I was home, Dimer and Sash had excitedly called from their new bazas in Washington and Toronto respectively. Many of the guys asked me about how Dimer was doing, but I was annoyed that few wanted to know about Godyniuk. Godyniuk was almost as popular on the club before leaving, but because of the nature of his taking off, it was no longer considered good form among team members to talk about him. They were backing Dimer all the way, hoping he would do well. Godyniuk, though, had violated the order of things. His wasn't a defection in the clear sense of the word as was Alexander Mogilny's. Mogilny had left the Soviet national team in Stockholm, following victory in the world championships there in 1989. With the escape, he had become the first hockey player in the forty-five-year history of the Soviets playing the game Western-style to defect.

The Japanese have a proverb on the theme of togetherness: "The nail that sticks up shall be hammered down." In the case of Godyniuk, he stuck up too far.

I was amazed while reading the book on Japanese baseball, *You Gotta Have Wa*, at the similarity of Soviet and Japanese attitudes toward sport. "Wa" means harmony, as in team harmony. It was demanded in Japan as in the Soviet Union in spades.

In Japan the players are required to live baseball in the way they live hockey here. Marriages, births, deaths—everything takes second place to training. The baseball system is one of commitment, discipline, control by the administration. Pain, suffering, hard work are the keys to the masterpiece. Through history there has been little interplay between the Japanese and Russian cultures—but by coincidence, the philosophy toward sport turned out the same.

Japanese baseball players are at the park ten hours a day. They approach their tasks, as author Robert Whiting reported, like assembly line workers at Toyota. It was not baseball but work-ball, and for the Russians, who approach their task in much the same way, it was not playing hockey so much as working hockey.

When asked the reason for his success, the legendary Japanese home run slugger Sadaharu Oh sounded much like the Russian great Tretiak. "I achieved what I did because of my coaches and my willingness to work hard," Oh said.

I could now identify with American baseball players going over to try to play the game in Japan. It wasn't such a traditional enemy culture as the Soviet one, but the differences were glaring and most American baseball players found the transition too difficult. While Soviet hockey had wider rinks, Japanese baseball had a wider strike zone. The officiating in each was different, as were the regimentation and the living conditions. In Japanese baseball you felt like you were in Sing Sing as well.

Warren Cromartie, a former Montreal Expo who did well in Japanese ball, said it takes "five months to get over the shock." My five months were more than over, but I wasn't sure about the shock.

Bogdanov remained aloof. He showed little interest in my vacation, wanting only to know how long I trained with the U.S. team, how many games I played, and how many goals I scored. Before the break I felt I had been making progress with this inscrutable man. With my limited ice time I wasn't scoring goals, but I was setting them up and my checking style was paying off in that the other team wasn't scoring goals when I was out there. I played with Vasilenko and different players on the other wing and it was basically understood that ours was the checking line. We did our job. My plus-minus rating at Christmas was among the best on the team.

But now it was like starting all over again. Bogdanov made me feel like a newcomer, to the point where I began to wish I hadn't taken the break from the team. It was like he was making me pay the price. At practice he put me on the fifth line, and again, for about the fourth time this year, he changed my position—now I would play center. He let me drift off, not really paying much attention to what I was doing. I wanted him to come straight—either I'm a full Soviet player or I'm out. I'd heard over Christmas about reports coming from Kiev back in September that I wasn't measuring up and that they were thinking of sending me home at that time. I must have showed them something in order to be kept on. But as my friends on the team told me, I wouldn't be back next year, so why would Bogdanov want to invest any time in me?

I didn't know if they were being honest or just trying to make me feel good. At any rate, after getting the fifth-line news I went to the scrimmage and played tough, scoring a goal and an assist.

In mid-January, as the U.S. deadline for war with Iraq approached, we received a major injection of perestroika. Our team was going private. Instead of a government-run operation we'd be a self-financed enterprise, sponsored by a local bank. It was part of a general trend toward self-financing begun a couple of years earlier as part of the Gorbachev reform campaign. The move seemed a highly significant development to me, but the players hardly thought it worth commenting on. I tried explaining that teams in the West were run this way and that it was the eventual key to a healthy, wealthy league. More operating money, high salaries, owners with fat cigars, I explained.

That pricked their ears some, but my projections suffered an early loss in credibility when we were told that the screws would be tightened even more—less expense money, less food, fewer sticks, less everything.

For the official changeover, we all had to sign new contract forms—two-page contracts in duplicate. It didn't strike me as a complicated task until I remembered it was the Soviet Union. There was only one copy of the contract for the entire team, and no copying machine! This meant it would have to be duplicated in longhand for each player. We were called to the dressing room where we were instructed to begin writing out the entire contract—twice. Twenty-five players from the Soviet Union's elite hockey division gathered around a small table and peered over one another's shoulders to copy it.

Yet one more time I was able to tell myself, "Welcome to the big leagues."

With all the austerity going on I accidentally pulled my Ugly American telephoning act again and felt like a real dick. I made a long long-distance phone call to Nikki with the guard on duty at the base monitoring it. When he announced with astonishment that the tab would be 180 rubles I shrugged it off like it was nothing. He then told me his salary was 80 rubles a month. I'd just used up the equivalent of almost two and a half months of his work pay on one phone call. I couldn't explain diplomatically that rubles to me were play dollars, or what my friends, Tim and Mark in Moscow, called Barney rubles. So I went with the line that with Nicole and me, the love was such that we'd bear any burden, pay any price to talk long distance.

The January 15 war-with-Iraq deadline day passed with me still in the dark. I was comforted to know, however, that there was no doubting the allegiance of the Sokol boys on this one. They were with team U.S.A. all the way. They didn't want war. There wasn't support for such a prospect in the Soviet Union the way there was in America, but if we had to go in, the Sokol boys were behind us.

Being more pacifist was a traditional Soviet boast, but I sensed such a quality among my teammates. Being a military superpower doesn't mean, as I somehow suspected, that the people are belligerent. The Soviets believed Saddam Hussein was wrong and supported Bush's position but hated to see it come to war. The legacy of World War II and its twenty-five million Soviet dead was still thick, and the Afghan experience wasn't far behind them. There were no Afghan vets on my team, but many players had friends who fought in the war.

Predictably, the most excited guy around the camp was Vasilenko, the Rambo man. He had been predicting all along that the Americans and the allies would wipe out Iraq in a hurry. Naturally he was the one to break the news of the opening of hostilities. Early on the morning of January 17, he made a beeline for my room to announce breathlessly that we were turning Iraq to rubble. Its air force was obliterated, as was Saddam's palace.

Vasily spread the news among all the team members and I got a few high-fives that day. My sense of what was going on was sketchy because I couldn't read Russian newspapers well enough yet and TV coverage was limited to two minute spots per day. But the players kept me abreast on the big stuff, and our victory only increased their awe of the American army and of the U.S.

The Soviets had their own remarkable leader in Gorbachev, who, for example, had got them out of Afghanistan. But to the players George Bush was the man. They, like the Soviet people generally, were so slow to trust their own leaders. The people had been beaten into submission and fooled too often in the past to have any remaining faith in the Communist party.

Foreign minister Eduard Shevardnadze had resigned, warning of a pending return to a dictatorship, but the Soviet families I knew didn't take this development at face value. They thought the move was just a ploy by Gorbachev that he and Shevardnadze had cooked up in advance. They were losing faith in Gorbachev. Glasnost was one thing, but the economy was another. It was worsening, and as it did they turned against him.

I didn't enjoy talking politics with the Soviets because it was depressing. They were always so negative. What joy they found was in their little private lives, far from the madding Communist crowd at the top.

One night, as darkness descended on the city, I was waiting for a bus in the gloom and the cold with several well-bundled Soviets. More arrived, among them many grandmas and grandpas and grandchildren. One of the grandfathers carried a little music box and turned it up when a Russian folk song came on. In the cold, he began to dance, and others formed into a semicircle and began to sing and dance with him. Some at the stop chose not to join in, but a warmth sped through the gathering and everyone was soon smiling. The moment became a vignette my mind would flash back to often. It suggested to me why the Soviets had been able to keep on despite all the dreadful dictatorships they had lived under.

It was only the next day that I boarded a bus and became totally confused about where I was heading. I knew I had to get off after the second bridge, but it was so crowded and the windows so fogged I could barely see out. Sensing my difficulty, a man with his wife and child helped, explaining I had several stops to go. I lost them after a while and was also losing count of the stops. Then I saw them coming again. They were preparing to get off but pushing their way past several people in order to reach me and tell me my stop would be two lights further.

When I got back to the base I was cold, and the non-working socialist workers, noticing this, were sympathetic but waved their forefingers at me for not wearing a hat. Not wearing a hat was difficult to get away with in the Soviet Union. All Russians wore them, and if you didn't, you heard about it—as I did so many times.

I went upstairs and about fifteen minutes later heard a knocking at the door. It was the workers. To warm me up they had prepared me a pot of hot tea and pastries.

It was true they didn't have anything else to do with their time. But they made good tea and I appreciated it and we talked about the war.

15

The hockey season in the USSR was progressing the way it had always progressed. The two clubs vying for the top ranking were Red Army and Dynamo Moscow. Likely no sport anywhere has been dominated so long by the same two teams. Between them, Red Army and Dynamo have won about 80 percent of the league championships since 1946.

Their mastery was only consistent with the order of things in the Soviet Union. What better symbols of power in the Soviet Union than the military and the KGB? Red Army was the military team, funded and run by the Department of Defense. Dynamo Moscow was the KGB team, sponsored and directed by the secret police and the militia in the Ministry of the Interior.

As well as running their sports teams, the army and police, the long-time pillars of Soviet repression, required the players to be members of their organizations.

To play on Red Army required the young athlete's becoming an officer of the Soviet army. To play on Dynamo required membership in the KGB or state militia. The commitment was usually for life, players on both teams making their post-hockey careers in the organizations.

I'd heard many stories about Americans, Canadians, and other Western athletes spooked by the thought of being followed around by the KGB while in the Soviet Union. Searching for wiretaps, they'd tear paintings from hotel rooms, pull up rugs from the floor, take telephones apart. One story had an athlete shouting "I've found it! I've found it!" when he discovered a fixture under his hotel room carpet. Hurriedly unscrewing the attachment to find the listening devices, he heard a crash and yelling in the room below. The chandelier, suddenly detached from the ceiling, had dropped on someone's dinner table.

Little did the visiting athletes know that the very spooks they feared were not hidden away in black coats, but in the case of the hockey players, often confronting them on the ice, nose to nose. Of course Dynamo players didn't act in an official spying capacity, but they did report to and were answerable to the KGB organization.

The tradition of army and secret-police supremacy in Soviet sport began early. After the 1917 Soviet revolution, private bourgeois sports clubs were disbanded and an effort was made to bring sport to the masses. Government-funded sports societies were established, among them the two that would produce the Soviet sportsmen who would topple all opposition in the Olympic Games. The Dynamo Sports Society was founded in

1923 by F. E. Dzerzhinsky, the head of Cheka, the fore-runner of the KGB. A few weeks later, the Central Army Sports Club was formed. Each began to operate sports schools at which, having plucked the best prospects in the country, they made a year-round effort to develop the students into stars. The army and the KGB networks were spread wider, had more funds than other Soviet organizations operating teams (mainly trade unions), and employed the additional weapon of intimidation.

I could picture the CIA and the Pentagon being given the mandate by Washington to develop sports training schools and to produce the best athletes and teams in football, baseball, hockey, etc., in the country. With our fantastic advantages in equipment, facilities, and sports technology, imagine the machines we could produce.

Red Army and Dynamo were essentially league all-star teams. Rising stars across the Soviet Union would soon be spotted and receive invitations to one of the two or both. The offers were not easy to turn down. Upward mobility in Soviet society was not secured by telling the army and the KGB where to get off.

Igor Larionov loved playing hockey in the small town of Voskresensk. He was a star there, knew everyone, and neighboring Moscow, huge and impersonal, had little appeal. Coach Tikhonov, however, wanted Larionov for his club. In Voskresensk one evening, a Red Army assistant took Larionov around the side of the arena where Tikhonov was waiting. "We want to invite you to our team," Tikhnov told the smallish centerman. "We have certain hopes tied up with you. With Army you will be fully able to discover your potential. You understand the situation?"

Larionov didn't say much, whereupon Tikhonov turned up the pressure. Even if he declined, "It is all the same. We will draft you into the army. Think it over Igor. Weigh it all carefully. We are talking, you know, about your future."

It was the way deals were made in Soviet hockey. Larionov had other offers. The coach of Spartak, also a Moscow team, took him to the Krause auto works, showed him thousands of cars spread across the fields like tanks, and told him if he joined Spartak, any one would be his. But Army offered the prospect of a post-hockey career and faster access to every Soviet player's goal—the national team. As well, there was the Tikhonov threat. Larionov joined.

Like Larionov, Helmut Balderis, the Soviet player so fast they dubbed him "Elektrichka" (electric train), joined Red Army under strong pressure from Tikhonov. He played a few seasons, but following the Olympic Games debacle in Lake Placid he wanted to return to play in his native Latvia where he began his career. Tikhonov told him if he left Red Army he would never again play for the national team. Balderis left and, despite outstanding seasons with the Riga team, was repeatedly left off the nationals. It was only years later when he led the Soviet league in scoring that, under strong pressure, Tikhonov named him to the national team.

Tikhonov held the rank of colonel. Among the Sokol players and others I met he was a feared and hated tyrant. When sufficiently angered he sometimes resorted to physical abuse. He skated over and punched Balderis at a practice once when the player shot a puck high that almost hit the goaltender in the head. In the 1988 Olympics Alexander Mogilny took a penalty in a meaningless game against the Finns. When he returned to the bench, Tikhonov slugged him in the stomach.

Most everyone outside the army organization hoped Tikhonov's team would lose. Even Dynamo was a more popular team. When the scores of games were announced in Soviet arenas, a loud cheer would go up whenever Red Army was trailing.

Tikhonov assembled his national team to represent the Soviet Union abroad almost entirely from his own Red Army team and Dynamo. Such was the case in Lake Placid in 1980 for the game that is still viewed by Soviets as the most inglorious moment in their hockey history and one of the worst in the history of Soviet sport. The loss to the U.S. came at a fever-pitch moment in cold war history—the Soviets had just invaded Afghanistan, and the Americans were boycotting the Moscow summer games.

It is a defeat still remembered vividly by Soviet hockey fans, and the verdict of history puts Viktor Tikhonov in the culprit's chair. His team was a colossal favorite. The Red Machine had been on a roll going into those games, many observers ranking that squad as the most talented Soviet hockey team ever. They'd beaten the NHL all-stars months earlier in New York 6–0, they'd swept through unbeaten in their own Izvestia tournament, and in an exhibition test they humiliated the U.S. Olympic team 10–3. The latter was the game in which Alexander Maltsev scored a goal skating backward. Moving quickly toward the net, Maltsev swept past Dave Christian, twirled, and from a position where the only goaltender he could see was his own (Tretiak) he shot the puck between the pipes. The goal scored backward was viewed as an appropriate symbol for the mismatch. The Olympics were supposed to be just as laughable.

As they look back today, the Soviets see the problems as beginning with the accommodations the Americans put them in. The Olympic village at Lake Placid was a converted federal penitentiary where the rooms were very small. Vladimir Yurzinov, then assistant coach, recalls that "Living in prison-style quarters took its toll on our players." He forgets to mention, however, that conditions for other teams were just the same and that if ever a team should have been prepared for prison-style living conditions it was the Russians.

Tretiak hated the living quarters and could not get comfortable during the games. Tikhonov was ill and not able to devote himself to his usual preparations for the game. Our coach, Herb Brooks, meanwhile had learned something at Madison Square Garden in the 10–3 loss. There, he sent only one forechecker in deep to the Russian zone. The tactic didn't work. It allowed easy breakouts, and once embarked on their attack, the Soviets were poison. What I was learning watching them now was that they were highly vulnerable if you got to them early, before they organized. Regularly, they would cough up the puck.

Brooks changed his strategy. A student of Tarasov, he remembered the Tarasov dictum—if you don't take the initiative, you don't win.

The Russians remember the end of the first period as the critical point in the game against the U.S. With the Soviets leading 2–1 and the buzzer about to sound, our

Dave Silk floated a shot in from the center red line that brought on two uncharacteristically derelict Soviet responses. First Tretiak allowed it to bounce off his pads out into play. Secondly, the defensemen, Dynamo players Pervukhin and Bilyaletdinov, outstanding players both, idled, thinking the stanza was over. Flying in between them came Mark Johnson. He gathered the loose puck and rifled it into the goal.

Tikhonov, beside himself with rage, went to the dressing room and made a decision he regrets to this day. He pulled Tretiak. The legendary goalie who had proved his worth a hundred times in the past was benched for one error.

The move was made under pressure. At every major international match, the Soviets would have several Kremlin officials in the stands. They would sometimes descend between periods and let their opinions be known to the coaches. In a famous incident in the world championships in Vienna in 1977, the head of the Soviet delegation fired the coach, Boris Kulagin, with a period remaining in the game against Sweden. The Soviets, needing a win for the gold, were trailing 2–1, a deficit that in the opinion of the delegation chief was the result of Kulagin's overly defensive approach. In the dressing room he ordered the assistant, Konstantin Loktev, to take over. Loktev obeyed but the Soviets still lost 3–1. New coaches were named shortly after the team returned home.

At Lake Placid, Tikhonov claims that "everybody advised me at that moment to replace Tretiak, and I unfortunately listened to their advice." Years later he was still lamenting the decision. "Of course it would have been risky to leave him in the game after such deplorable mistakes. But the risk would have been justified. In this great player is an incredible strength of willpower. With my decision I really insulted him and singled him out unfairly. Afterward I apologized."

Pulling Tretiak created a crisis atmosphere on the Soviet team while instilling new confidence in the Americans. The USSR still led 3–2 after the second period, but Tikhonov, always a highly emotional coach, was panicking and made another strategic blunder. Throughout the final frame, he went with tired veterans against Brooks's swift collegians. It was a strange choice. Tikhonov had usually leaned to young legs. He was the first Soviet coach ever to use four lines, pioneering the system while coaching in Riga. It proved successful and is now used, almost unfailingly, by every other Soviet coach.

But in the final period at Lake Placid, it was Herb Brooks who moved to four lines and new reserves of energy while Tikhonov went almost half the period with the over-thirty gang of Mikhailov, Petrov, and Kharlamov. They couldn't keep up. Swift young Soviet reserves, brilliant stars of the future like Makarov and Krutov, languished on the bench. Myshkin, the new goalie, let in two goals that Tretiak might well have stopped. Then in the final minutes Tikhonov appeared to lose his sense of the game. Petrov looked to the bench like he was pleading for a break for his weary trio. But Tikhonov waved them back on. Trailing by one, it was imperative that Tikhonov get his goalie out for an extra attacker. But he appeared not even to think of it. He never once looked in Myshkin's direction. Brooks couldn't believe his good fortune.

The United States still had to defeat Finland for the gold medal. The Russians came to the rink for their game against Sweden while the match against the Finns was in progress. "It was 2–1 in favor of the Finns when we arrived and started dressing for our game," recalled Yurzinov. "Then we heard the noise from the stands and we understood that the Americans had tied the game and moved ahead to win. I looked at the eyes of our players and I had never seen eyes like that before. Some of them were so heartsick that, instead of putting on their game uniforms, they mistakenly put on their practice jerseys. They didn't know what they were doing."

In this and in other vital contests, the Soviets had no end game. Their record in the most important games was poor. They lost the gold to the U.S. not only in 1980 but in 1960 at Squaw Valley. The only times they lost to the Americans in that twenty year span were those two gold-medal games. They'd also lost in the final seconds of the historic 1972 series against Canada. They lost the major confrontation with the Stanley Cup champion Philadelphia Flyers in 1976, and they lost, again in closing seconds, the sensational finales of the Canada Cup in 1984 and 1987.

Their repressive hockey system had built marvelous technicians, players whose skill level was superior. But there was nothing more. With the emphasis on the collective, with the Japanese thing about no nails sticking out, they could not find new levels of intensity, the emotional overdrive that carried Americans and Canadians beyond their natural abilities.

Robotic to the end, leaderless because their system didn't want leaders, the Russians couldn't play climax hockey. They couldn't win on what Wayne Gretzky said the Canadians won on in 1987—guts alone.

Alexander Yakushev, a former Soviet star who now coaches Spartak, recognized the problem. "There is something that is missing in European players in general and in the Soviet players in particular. It's called fighting to the very end."

Having seen the spirit sucked out of them by the imposed conformity of the old revolution, by a league that was dominated by such forces as the army and the KGB, I was curious to see whether the new liberties would put a little kick back in their systems. But judging by the on-ice look of the even-keel Sokol boys, the break from the socialist torpor would be long in coming.

For all the glasnost and all the other changes perestroika was bringing, at the hockey level the old guard was still in control. Ten years after the Lake Placid disaster the two coaches who presided over the team there, Tikhonov and Yurzinov, still held the reins. Despite great public feuds with players, despite players bolting to the NHL, despite repeated calls for his resignation, Tikhonov, now sixty, clung to the army and national team portfolios. Yurzinov, who served as Tikhonov's assistant on the national team for a decade, coached Dynamo to the 1989–90 championship and looked a good bet to repeat.

Around the Sokol camp Yurzinov was regarded as the best coach in the league, and there was talk of him succeeding Tikhonov as national team coach. It would be tantamount to one KGB man succeeding another. Yurzinov had spent almost his entire career, both as player and coach, in the Dynamo organization. Tikhonov first played in the early 1950s on the air force team that was run by Joseph Stalin's son, Vasily. Then he joined Dynamo Moscow where he played for a decade before moving to Riga to coach the Dynamo team there.

Owing to the perestroika pressures of the times the two men had to make some changes in their modus operandi. But fundamentally they were Stalin-era communists who, not wanting any part of Gorbachev's new thinking, demanded player discipline and isolation. "I think glasnost is making headway too fast," Yurzinov stated. "Our players have more free time—and what is the result? They aren't training better, they aren't working better, and they don't play better. Maybe it is a new time, but is it a better or worse time?"

Yurzinov remembered fondly the old days when idealism pervaded Soviet society and was reflected in the fanatical dedication of the players. Players today "are simply forgetting what the coach does for them," he said. "In your country there has never been a coach who has done as much for his players as our coaches have done for ours. In our country the coach is like a father and mother combined. He takes care of everything for the players."

But the Soviet players didn't want that. Where had it gotten them? They looked abroad and saw a system light-years ahead of their own. Under the Tikhonovs and the Yurzinovs, Soviet hockey had gone the route of the rest of Soviet society through the Brezhnev years: stagnation, decay, boredom. The system of army-KGB domination of the sport created a predictability that saw the game's popularity tumble. Thousands of youths once vied to get into a hockey school like Dynamo's or Army's. Now the numbers were down to a trickle. In a cold-weather country the size of the Soviet Union, with three hundred million people, the idea that there could only be one hundred covered hockey rinks seemed almost unimaginable.

The country that put the first rockets in outer space still couldn't produce better than third-world sports equipment. I arrived for one of our games in January to see Sherayev, the man with the K for captain on his jersey, a sometimes national team player, sitting with a needle and thread trying to mend holes in his hockey socks. After Khristich and Godyniuk left, the two replacements who were called up were given Khristich's and Godyniuk's equipment—skates and uniforms. They were told the hand-me-downs would have to do. There was no extra new stuff. One of the players tried Khristich's skates, but they were a horrible fit and he finally gave up and went back to his old ones, which were falling apart.

The reason Soviet players were being allowed to be sent abroad had a lot to do with Gorbachev's glasnost. But it also had to do with the fact that the hockey teams were so desperate for foreign currency to purchase decent equipment that they felt they had no choice.

The Sokol boys could look forward to better stuff in 1991 because the word was that the proceeds from the Khristich deal netted the team a hundred thousand dollars. With Western sports teams the amount would be a smidgen; here it was a bonanza.

Performance bonuses for the Sokol players were usually doled out in rubles. Now it would be dollars. Bogdanov, who was getting desperate for more wins, explained the new deal. His rating of each player on a per-game basis was a maximum of five and a minimum of one. In order to get the new dollar bonuses the team first had to win the game. A five rating in that case would net a player seventy-five dollars. A four was worth sixty dollars, a three forty-five dollars, and so on.

The dollar system was top secret, to be known only to the players and their immediate families. If the hockey fathers in Moscow ever found out, I was told, there would be a lot of trouble. A player told me not to talk about any of it on the phone because the KGB might be listening in.

With the dollar signs ringing, the team began to show more spark and togetherness. Sherayev used the bucks as an incentive in pep talks between periods. Soon, I thought, he might be able to get a new pair of hockey socks.

In late January we beat Torpedo Yaroslavl and Dynamo Riga and were feeling good. But the money incentive wasn't enough to carry us past club Yurzinov or club Tikhonov. We started out well in both games, but in the end the natural order of things reasserted itself. The tradition, begun in 1923, continued. The military and the KGB teams won handily.

16

I n Ust-Kamenogorsk, where the Sokol boys would pull back their eyes in slant formation, mocking the Kazakh population, the shelves in the stores showed bread, honey, canned tomatoes, juice, butter, canned cabbage, fish, chicken, and beef. The offerings were hardly sumptuous and there was not much in the way of choice. American consumers, given their customary cornucopia, no doubt would find the stores terribly wanting, an attitude that perhaps explained why the Soviet situation was being portrayed so bleakly in the Western media—as if there were a famine of some kind. There was no famine. Gorki and a couple of cities I visited certainly offered grim prospects for the food shopper, but not desperation.

The Soviets felt let down because perestroika had fired their expectations to unattainable proportions. The fantastic surge in political liberties that they could now enjoy didn't compensate for the lack of Western goods.

The people were calling Gorbachev the sly fox now, saying he was only acting to keep himself in power, and they were losing faith in Boris Yeltsin as well. Extraordinary. Even Gorbachev and Yeltsin, the two leading Soviet reformers, could not find favor with these people. The Soviets wanted an economic miracle—and until a politician delivered it, they would be dissatisfied.

In the meantime though, this was a population well acquainted with privation, one that knew how to tough it out. Because of shortages, the lineups had worsened, but it was still all rather routine for the luckless Russians, and as the winter wore on, they joked and made do. Everywhere I traveled I never failed to see fresh flowers for sale. Outside the store in Ust-Kamenogorsk, children with rosy cheeks skated on ice-covered streets or skied cross-country or slid down snow-covered hills on their bottoms.

Back home in Kiev I was cheered by the likes of Igor, a worker at the base, and his wife Lana. Though married many years, Igor and Lana still remained billeted with Lana's parents due to the housing shortage. Igor appeared to be more industrious than the average non-working socialist at the base and at home was a handyman, always fixing things. Lana worked hard on learning English. They were typically lacking in possessions but knew how to enjoy life. They would go for motorcycle rides, picnics in the forest, the movies, dancing, skiing, or running in the snow with their dog Ren. They made great shish kebabs. Like other Soviets they relied on one another for entertainment instead of a box with an electronic screen in it. I was reading about a U.S. diplomat who came to Moscow with his son. The kid missed television so much he became totally unmanageable.

Igor and Lana invited me over one night. Because of the cramped conditions they offered to sleep on the living room floor and let me have their bedroom. Again, the thought that ran through my mind was, how many Americans would do this for a visiting Soviet? I declined the offer and spent the rest of the evening trying politely to turn down other ones. The knitted wall hanging depicting a dog, for example: Lana, who had made it herself, said she wanted me to have it. I declined but made the mistake of mentioning that I needed to buy a hat. In a minute out came a hat, courtesy of Igor. "No need to buy one, Tod. Take this." We had tea, talked, played songs on the guitar, and danced to some of their tapes.

I went to the movies with them one February night, and even though I was the one with the money, they insisted on paying. Like other Soviets, Igor and Lana were almost impossible to pry yourself from. After the movie they wanted me to stay overnight. The team wasn't at the base but nonetheless I wanted to get back to write letters, relax, read. They were visibly hurt as I tried to explain in fumbling Russian what I had to do. What I wanted to say was that although it was really boring at the camp, I had to get back because I had a lot to do. But I went away mortified because I think what I said was, "Thanks, but staying at the camp isn't as boring as staying with you people."

After practice the next day, however, I returned to my room and found that Igor and Lana had left me pie and apples and a jar of compote. Whatever I said couldn't have upset them too much. Also there were apples and a jar of juice from the daughter of the manager of the team.

February 23 was Army Day in the Soviet Union. Igor and the workers at the base had their traditional little celebration for the war veterans among them—Nikolai the director and Anatole. The women who worked with them prepared a buffet of sausage, cheese, potatoes, bread, oranges, juice, candy, and vodka. Everyone held his glass forward and toasted time after time as the two vets spoke of their service years. They were distant memories of four and half decades ago but still close enough to bring these men to tears.

I was just there as a curious spectator, but the women presented me with a flower and a bottle of cologne. This day was for former Soviet soldiers, not young American hockey players. But I was the first American to break the Soviet hockey barrier, they announced, and was therefore an honorary soldier. The recognition was moving.

The novelty of my being here was wearing off among Soviet fans. In Leningrad, where they had a pathetic team, there were shouts of "Hartje go home, Hartje go home!" I felt like yelling back, "I wish I could! I wish I could!" It was the only city in which I heard negative feedback, and in response I bloodied a guy's nose and almost touched off a brawl.

Oddly enough, one of my favorite stops on the circuit was Ust-Kamenogorsk, the place the Sokol boys disdained. I was delighted on my return trip there to see the young boy who had presented me with the five-kopeck piece my first time through. He was waiting for me, his big wondrous eyes an invitation to a hundred stories that the language barrier would not let us share.

A man who looks after the rink there came over and asked if I would trade hats because he would be thrilled to have one with English writing on it. In Voskresensk I had turned down the Russian rink rat who wanted to trade jackets, so this time I let my hat go.

A noisy crowd came out to the game, at which a couple of Ust-K players sported photos of Gretzky on their helmets, and generated the excitement some Western crowds do. Even though I sat on the bench I enjoyed that game. Skating around between periods, I heard a voice ring down from the rafters: "Hartje, do you speak English?"

While liking this city and the Kazakh people, I was dismayed by our teams attitude. In this part of the country you could really get a sense of the racism in the Russians. Blacks, Asians, and Jews were the targets. On our flight, one of the team members nudged me on the side while looking over his shoulder to the back of the plane. A black was sitting there. I ignored my teammate, but he persisted and finally getting my attention said, "Black! black!" Then in Russian, "Chorny! chorny!"

At the hotel I mentioned I liked a song that was on the radio. One of the guys interjected, "No, no, bad song." "What are you talking about?" I asked. "Kazakh, Kazakh," he responded.

The Russians particularly looked down on the people in the southern republics. Because their skin coloring was different, they were deemed inferior. With the Ukrainians, our Russian players were comparatively harmonious, and I never heard our players curse the people from the Baltic states. The further west a population was located, the more the Russians respected them. But I don't think the average Russian would have given a damn if the republics to the south split from the union.

At a birthday party I met George from the republic of Georgia, who was with a three-hundred-pound drinking buddy. The more we drank the more all of us could understand one another and the more I could understand the power of the nationalist sentiment among Georgians. George stunned me after all this, however, by declaring he was married to a Russian.

He had surprised himself too, he said. "But what can you do when you fall in love. You marry her—even if she's a Russian."

Georgia was where the reputed big-time Soviet mafiosi hung out. The Mafia was spread far and wide in the country and was taken very seriously by the likes of the players on my hockey team. I first found this out when I stood up in a restaurant to take a picture of several men dressed in black at a corner table. Three of my teammates dragged me down, telling me I was out of my mind. At dinner in Gorki, a group of about fifteen, all in black hats and black leather jackets, sat at the next table while the Sokol boys cowered. The players made a special point of watching out for me—not even letting me go off to the bathroom by myself. The guys in the corner were the real thing, they said. They were beginning to run Soviet cities like Chicago was run by the hoods of the 1930s.

I never saw any violence, but in Moscow one night a Mafia group forcibly entered a restaurant and surrounded a table. The thug they talked to got up angrily from his seat only to be shoved back down into it. The

Mafia characters in this bunch looked particularly young. Many were ex-athletes, my teammates told me. They had nothing to do after their careers, so they teamed up with gangsters.

Tikhonov was always being compared to a Mafia don by our players because of his use of threats. The latest involved the bright young star Kozlov from Khimik Voskresensk. He had been fingered by Tikhonov and would be joining Red Army after the season. Kozlov had decided to cooperate, everyone suspected, because if he didn't, Tikhonov would keep him off the national team.

The hockey don was in need of performers like Kozlov because Dynamo Moscow was on a roll again and threatening to repeat as champions. The word was that a drinking epidemic had hit Red Army and that Tikhonov, exhausted with the turmoil of recent years, had turned a blind eye to it.

Our club meanwhile was playing sub-.500 hockey; among the ten teams that advanced after Christmas, we were plodding along in eighth place. We continued as we had most of the year—beating the low-ranking teams, losing to the league powers. None of the Sokol boys were down about it because, as I have noted, this was the order of things. In their minds they were not supposed to do better. The one time we beat Dynamo Moscow was true cause for celebration. Champagne was opened in the dressing room. Bogdanov walked over to me. Raising a glass, he laughed, "Just like Stanley Cup, eh?"

Since returning from the Christmas break I had been used mostly as a pinch hitter, replacing whoever on the club was having a bad game. It meant playing all over the place, oftentimes only for a few shifts a game. I wanted more playing time, but I was getting enough out of this journey, from the point of view of both culture and hockey knowledge, to keep going. Any thought I had of coming over here and being some kind of star performer—and I never really had such a thought—was long gone.

But I bet I had learned much more about life since the summer than most college grads my age. Back home my month of January would have been tied up with thoughts of the Super Bowl. We were entering March over here now and I still had no idea who won the Super Bowl and I hardly cared. Thoughts had turned instead to a new continent, a new culture, a new life, broader perspectives. Whether I was enjoying this experience was not the question. The question was one of personal growth, and in that I knew I was succeeding. It was the first thing Nicole noticed when she came over. I could talk intelligently about a range of subjects that a year before would never have crossed my mind.

Nicole finally arrived after some ridiculous Western media hype about turmoil here had almost scared her into staying home. Friends back home were advising her, on the basis of the reports, that it was unsafe. Unsafe to come to Kiev? This was the most stupid thought I'd heard in months. There was no sense of crisis here, nor in other cities. It was only from talking to people in the United States that I, the one who was here, heard about the supposed turmoil.

Nikki wanted to go and give Bogdanov hell for the way he was using me, but I kept her away from him, knowing this type of thing just wasn't done. She sat up in the stands with the players' wives listening to their constant bitching about not being able to see their husbands. This confirmed my impression that the wives were more bothered by it than the Sokol boys themselves.

Bogdanov was generous in that he let me spend a lot of time with Nik—certainly more than the other players spent with their girlfriends. Nikki, too, was overwhelmed by the generosity of the Soviets, her preconceptions being altered almost to the degree mine had been.

In search of American food, we ate at Pizza Hut in Moscow. We were going to try McDonald's but the line was two blocks long, stretched two and three across. At Pizza Hut we could have been served right away in the foreign currency queue but did it the Russian way, standing in the ruble line outside in the sleet and rain. Tourists looked at us like we were crazy, but you couldn't beat the price—three rubles a slice, about fifteen cents American. And it tasted the same as it did at home.

While letting Nikki and me spend a lot of time together, Bogdanov didn't break with his system of segregating women from the team. In Moscow he wouldn't let the two of us stay in the same hotel as the rest of the team.

We were finding actually that the separation was good for us. Our love was growing stronger. We had tested it. We had split to separate continents for the better part of the year at an age when anything can happen and found that the distance brought us closer. The Russian women, as beautiful and as giving as some were, hadn't broken our bond. I don't think I knew what love was until I had spent such a long time away from it. It's a test I'd recommend to many.

Kuzy, my buddy on the team who like me had decided to tie the knot, had spent a great deal of time away from his fiancée, even though they lived in the same city. Having let me in on his marriage plans a few months earlier, he now came to me again with his signal phrase for pending big news. "Tod," he intoned, looking me square in the eye, "We have bizzness."

It was during a practice. We sought out a private corner of the ice. "Yeah, Kuz, what's up."

"Tod, my wedding. I want you be best man mine."

I wasn't sure about the wisdom of the choice but was flattered. The wedding, I was pleased to learn, wasn't until the end of the season. During the season it would have been tough. I'd heard Russian weddings usually took about a fortnight to recover from. The booze shipments for Kuzy's nuptials were already beginning to arrive. They had to stockpile over an extended period of time in order to have enough. You could only buy so many bottles at one time.

I would be with the team until April, when I would join Team U.S.A. for the Pravda Cup tournament in Leningrad. The Pravda Cup featured top teams from the international hockey powers, with the Soviets usually sending their second-ranked all-star team. Being picked for the American squad gave me a shot of pride. I wanted Bogdanov to hear about it, so I asked him about the makeup of the Soviet team in order to get in a discussion about it.

As the season wore down, the crowds were getting large and the league picked up in excitement. Despite the increased attendance the money situation on our team was grave and Bogdanov felt compelled to miss a game and several days of practice to go on the road trying to line up more sponsors. We got a break when the Sports Palace managers decided not to charge rent for the remainder of the season. Otherwise we would have had to play the games in our small practice rink.

Before he left Bogdanov held two meetings—one for the veteran players, one for the young. This was in keeping with his policy of dividing the team into two spheres. He ripped into the players for showing no character, heart, desire, leadership, and just about everything else. For the umpteenth time, the young skaters were told how bleak the prospects for the team would be when the veterans retired. It was the no-one-to-pass-the-torch-to lecture. Again he went around to all the players, asked about their failures, and demanded what they were going to do about them. Most American coaches would do this one-on-one number in private in the office. With Bogdanov, praise, punishment, and disputes were handled publicly.

One of the guys in trouble was Sasha Savetsky. Through the season I had become closer to his parents than Sav himself. Sav and I got along, but we didn't meet the real test of friendship—we didn't have the urge to learn about one another. His parents wanted me over all the time, however, and sometimes I'd go and spend the evening with them while Sav went out drinking with the guys. His parents bought me a Christmas gift, but by the time I appeared at their place to collect it it was late January. No matter. They still had a Christmas tree up with the sole present under it.

Their son was not a terribly disciplined player and was more openly hostile to Bogdanov than the rest. His ice time waned as the season progressed. I could sense something was wrong with Mrs. Savetsky one night as we returned from the Sports Palace but reasoned she was just tired from starting work at seven in the morning and going to the rink directly afterward. At home she told me she wanted to talk secretly.

Why was her son not getting ice time, she asked. Why was he in trouble with the coach? She began to cry. I told her that problems with the coach were routine on the team and that Sav would pull out of it. I wanted to tell Sav how worried he was making his mother—but our conversation was secret.

Sav lacked intensity, didn't backcheck and didn't crash the enemy zone. In short he had the common deficiencies of most Soviet players. In talks with some of them, including Sav, I would suggest these problems, but a change in the essential character of how they played was not going to happen quickly.

In studying the play of the Russians I was always jotting formulas for beating them. It was the only spying I did on the entire excursion. As a sign of the changing times I wasn't even briefed by the CIA. My list of ways to beat the Russians? Stay out of the box defense. Fill their passing lanes. Backcheck like men possessed. Jump on their defense early, before they get started. Be ready for the high zone passes. Finish your check by taking the player with the body, so he can't come back into the play quickly. Crash the net on offense—they give up precious space in the slot area. Show respect but don't be intimidated. Kill them with emotion.

Soviets were complacent hockey players. We tied Khimik 3–3 and were happy about it. They were the fifth place team and we were playing at home but were happy about the tie. We led Spartak 3–1 after two periods only to give up three goals in the third and lose it 4–3. At home against Soviet Wings, the third place team, we were leading 2–0 after two and kept it halfway through the third. They scored two late goals to get the tie. I thought everybody would have been pissed, but they were delighted with the draw. Bogdanov came in and congratulated us.

I did manage to inject a degree of intensity into a workout during a return trip to Gorki, where, thankfully, a new arena had been erected. We were doing a five-on-five drill, a hockey version of a game of keepaway, when I smashed Eduard Valiulin so hard into the boards that he came back at me. When he did I rammed him again with my shoulder. We started throwing punches, or in his case, pawing punches. Most of these players had little or no experience fighting and Eduard was one of them. He didn't even throw his gloves off. Consequently the fight didn't amount to much, but it was still a big deal for a Kiev hockey practice.

I was annoyed it happened because I was highly sensitive to the problem of the American coming over and causing trouble. I didn't want to give added credence to the notion, albeit a correct one, that ours was a more violent culture than the Soviet one. In the Soviet Union, every second family doesn't own a handgun.

On the bus trip back from practice, Valiulin came up from behind and in a friendly gesture tapped me on the shoulder, obviously wanting to make up. We both started joking about it.

It was one of the few occasions I stirred any trouble. Another involved my taping of the coach's lectures. I would play back the tapes, especially the rantings of Teapot, and the players would get a great kick out of it. A couple of hours before a game Bogdanov walked in on one of these sessions—we were all howling at Teapot's commands—and was not amused. He switched it off and launched into a speech about the need for a more serious attitude. He knew it was me playing the tape.

While our team's destiny was a totally unremarkable seventh or eighth place, Bogdanov took these stakes to be highly significant. Noticeable was the more frequent use of the yellow pills. I didn't know what they were called. I just knew from a couple of the players that they gave you an incredible surge of energy. Even Doc wouldn't tell me about them. "Secret," he said. "Big secret." He offered them to me and I declined, as did several of the other players. But those who took them testified to their power. Kuzy, normally an abstainer, said his eyes would start bulging like they were going to pop out. Right through to the following morning he said he could feel the surge.

The yellow pills were not the only thing the coach brought out in the final days. Bogdanov was tight. We had to win our final game against Torpedo Yaroslavl to finish seventh. So he made his final plea bargain. A victory, he said, would be worth a week off from training. A loss and the players would have to report back in two days, as previously scheduled.

I laughed. The new season wouldn't begin until September, and yet they were requiring the Sokol boys to report back to training two days after the season ended in late March. With a win, a break was possible—for a whole week!

The bonus offer wasn't enough to shake up the Sokol boys. We tied 1–1 and ended up eighth. It was a disappointing finish, but the feeling in the dressing room after this game was hardly different from that after any other. The main subject of discussion was not the game, but where to go drinking.

17

The general manager for the Washington Capitals telephoned me, wanting to talk about Khristich. My old pal Dimer, gone to the NHL, experiencing my culture jump in reverse, was in a royal red funk, so much so that he didn't want to play for the Caps anymore.

Not knowing that practical jokes are an alien concept in the USSR, the Caps had played one on Dimer. They filled his shoes with ketchup—right up to the brim.

Dimer saw it as a serious insult, not a joke. The Caps players disliked him, he felt. This was their way of showing it.

Players tried to explain, but Dimer wasn't prepared to listen. He wouldn't talk to anyone on the team. He told management that when Hartje went to play for Sokol Kiev he was treated with respect by everyone and invited to their homes and well taken care of.

A meeting with the coach, the general manager, and

the captains of the team was held. It was explained to Khristich that this was the type of thing frequently done to new players in the NHL. It was tradition, in the spirit of fun. The players were sorry but Dimer should understand that they're his friends and didn't think of the possibility the joke would be misinterpreted.

Dimer still wasn't moved. "If they my friends, why do this? Why ruin my shoes?" This was another aspect. The Soviets, used to so little, were so careful and guarded with their possessions. For the typical NHLer one pair of shoes was nothing. For the Russian, it was sometimes the only pair he had.

The Caps had called me earlier, at Christmas when Khristich first joined them, to ask for suggestions to ease his transition. Washington already had one Russian on their team. The talented, beefy, hard-shooting defenseman Mikhail Tatarinov had recently arrived and was playing well but not fitting smoothly into the Caps system of operations.

I told John Perpich, the team's assistant coach, that it was most important that Dimer got involved, that his schedule was full, that he be made to feel part of the team. Soviet players were used to having their lives orchestrated, dictated by the police-state coach. If they landed, untutored, in America, suddenly free of high command, they would have problems.

What I hoped was that the generosity of Soviet society toward foreigners would be reciprocated by Americans. I didn't think though of telling them that practical jokes weren't understood.

When I spoke to Dimer on the phone, I pointed out that the ketchup anecdote was one of the many cultural differences he would have to try and bridge. I think the talk softened him some, but he was still slow in coming round. The NHL playoffs were on and the Caps, who had been pleased with Dimer's performance, needed him at his best.

At the Sokol camp meanwhile I was preparing to take my leave. There was Kuzy's wedding, the team banquet, the final goodbyes, then I would be on to Leningrad to join my fellow Americans in the Pravda Cup, playing against the Russians instead of for them.

At the final practice with the team, I didn't want to leave the ice. I continued to skate while the others slowly drifted off to the dressing room or what I always referred to now as the razdevalka, the Russian term for it.

One player lingered with me. He was the guy who had stopped along the roadway that hot day in July when my bicycle broke down and helped me get started again. Vasily Vasilenko became my first Soviet friend then, and throughout the season I remained close to Sokol's American military expert. As we took a final skate together, I could feel a closeness to him and a comfort in being with him that was reserved for the closest of my friends back home. Rambo told me I was his best friend on the team. "Tod," he said in a questioning tone. "I will see you in America some day?"

I heard that same thought so often in my final days, expressed with just a tinge of optimism. They wanted to start new lives and do so in a Western country. There was Andrei Ovchinikov, a defenseman. His father was the mayor of Kiev and I expected Andrei would have passions beyond hockey, especially given the revolutionary currents sweeping his country. But Andrei only had one dream—to go to live and play hockey in North America. He had spent some weeks in Canada with the Soviet national junior team and fallen in love with the place. "I will see you in Winnipeg some day?" he asked. Compared to Kiev, physically at least, Winnipeg was a backwater. But of course for Andrei, it wasn't a question of beauty. There were other values more important to him than aesthetic ones.

Then there was Vika, Vika with her soft brown patriotic eyes on her elegant slender frame. She didn't belong in the United States. Her country, be it the Ukraine or some Soviet version of it, needed her heart and will. As the season progressed, however, Vika's layers of pure Slav woman were peeled back to reveal a disillusionment that was profound and puzzling. Like so many others, at the very moment her society was breaking from the chains, she grew distraught and despaired, and wanted to get away to a new beginning.

For her, change was coming too slowly and it was too doubtful. At the school where she taught, the master was still making her instruct the students in the Lenin drivel that they had been learning for decades. Gorbachev's midwinter swerve to the right had depressed her more. I hoped that maybe I had just caught her on a bad day and the spark hadn't truly gone out from her, because this was a kind, kind soul who from my initial faulty impression of her as a team groupie had emerged as something special. She was curious in that she loved hockey like most women loved flowers. Her will was as hard as ice, and although her country needed her, I felt it not unlikely that we would cross paths in the United States some day.

Kuzy's wedding was a gas. It started in Richard Nix-on's limo. Somehow the limo that Brezhnev had driven during the 1972 summit, terrifying Richard Nixon in the process, had found its way to Kiev. The Sokol boys rented it out for special occasions and this was one of them.

Young Kuzy was cool about the day, much cooler than I. I had little knowledge of Russian wedding conventions and feared I would screw up the protocol.

As we left Kuzy's house, having watched *Beverly Hills Cop* on TV the night before, Kuzy's mom stood outside tossing coins and candy in the air to neighbors who wished him good luck. It was then our duty, that of the groom and best man, to go to the home of the father of the bride. The father could either say no, and hand the rejected suitor a watermelon, or yes, and present him with a bouquet. As Kuzy joked, had the old man wanted to present a watermelon he wouldn't have been able to find one in Kiev anyway.

The procession of cars sped downtown to an office building where they churned out newlyweds like they were coming off a conveyor belt. The same wedding tune blared through the windows time after time, the sound quality that of a scratchy LP.

When our turn came, a very communist-looking woman led us into a nondescript room where another charwoman stood behind an altar, nothing godly around her neck, only a Communist party medal. She stared at us all in an intimidating way and said a few words, to which Kuzy and Natasha each responded, "Da." Then Tanya and I spread a towel out in front of them on the floor. The bride and groom stepped forward onto it, and

229

rings were brought forward and exchanged. The bride got to keep the towel they stood on, there were more words I couldn't understand, then kisses, bows, congratulations, pictures.

Outside champagne toasts followed, then that fine tradition of smashing your glass into the ground, then it was off to consume crates of alcohol. Toast upon toast upon toast upon toast. The hockey coaches were at the reception, joining in the bacchanalia in full measure and showing themselves to be very different men than at the camp. Now their Stalinist masks were off, and loosened by the liquor they became as human as the next guy. Teapot even performed a Ukrainian dance.

Many peculiar observances took place, the meaning of which I was too blitzed to find out. Kuzy held out a string of beads and pushed them to the other end of the string while mouthing words like love, health, devotion. Natasha then pushed them back, rhyming off the names of animals as she did so. A cabbage was presented to them and they ripped it in half, part of a preplanned routine.

I stayed at Kuzy's house that night with members of the wedding party and woke up totaled, my head like a bowling ball with sirens wailing inside. When the assembled chalk-faced hosts saw me, they pronounced me ill. I didn't disagree, whereupon someone announced, "Dis no problem. I have just dee cure."

Oh shit, I thought, and as I expected out came the vat of samogon, that deadly, ghastly Soviet home brew. I said no a thousand times, but they filled a glass the size of a wastepaper basket and poured it down me like lemonade. "Dis good. Now you feel better. Da?"

Then somebody's uncle showed up with a quart of purply alcohol so strong it was screaming from the bottle. My insides, which were already a volcano, were now drenched with this gasoline. Dreadful Ukrainian folk music pounded at an ultradecibel range, all this at 9:30 in the morning. They were just beginning their day. I felt like I was just ending my life.

Before I could recover from the wedding, we had a repeat performance—the season-ending team banquet; only at this one, I couldn't last any longer than 10:30 P.M. Too wrecked to continue, I was stuffed by the Sokol boys into a car and sent back to the base. In my hockey season in the Soviet Union I had learned a few things Soviet, but no matter how much I practiced there was one thing I couldn't learn—how to drink Russian-style. At this game they were the masters. In the blood, I suppose. One thousand years of custom.

I said teary goodbyes to most of the players and their families individually. The morning I was to leave for Leningrad to play for the Americans in the tournament, everyone assembled down in the main hall of the residence. Bogdanov spoke first. In the days prior we had spoken to one another frequently, and during these chats, too late, far too late, I grew to like this man and respect his intelligence. He was personable, sensitive, smart.

Now he spoke to the players and carefully avoided the subject of my hockey. What he said was how I had broken the barrier, how I had fit in so well and become liked by so many. Not easy under the conditions I faced coming in, he told the players, but it was done. "Good boy," he said, "a good boy." Then he gave me a big hug, an embrace that made me feel good because there was genuine warmth, lots of warmth.

Having already said private words to most of the guys, I didn't add much now. I recalled my nervousness when I arrived and talked about how they had accepted me and how we had developed a bond. "So many Americans told me that this couldn't happen," I said to them, "that our culture, our history, our cold war rivalry had made us so different that something like my relationship with you guys, a relationship of love and trust, was impossible. But we proved them wrong, we proved that Soviets and Americans can be one, can live together.

"Good luck with your country," I concluded. "I hope to see you all in five years."

I don't know why I said five years. I just assumed at the rate things were moving it would take that long before the divisions were really down. No one knew the new revolution was only a few months away—though there was plenty talk about a possible coup.

I shook everyone's hand, and then, this being five months before the opening of their new season and just after the end of the old, they went out for their first training session of the day—the 10K run.

I had a last word with Igor the hockey fanatic. His last name, I finally found out, was Vakalyk. He was Ukrainian and somewhat of a nationalist. "When I get to America," he said, "the pronunciation will be Vikuluk. This is the Ukrainian pronunciation. I will change it then."

He reflected about a few things. "You are an American player, so we were very interested in everything about you. We believe our country is opening up when our most proud sport of hockey permits an American to join. Many people thought your arrival was for advertising purposes because our attendance was going downhill. So Sokol wanted something different for the fans.

"But as well as the novelty value," Igor said, "I think the fans liked you for the energy you gave. We don't normally get to watch players who work so hard every shift."

Igor saw the situation in his country as coming to a head. "I am a military officer but I am against communism. If the Baltic people want their independence they should be granted it. In our region we want independence too. We are worried that Moscow will use chemical weapons and tanks against us."

Like so many others, Igor the hockey fanatic had become a believer in the American dream. "I don't believe them [the politicians] when they tell us some day we will live as the Americans do. It is too much to hope for.

"At school we were taught that Americans were the enemy number one. You have shown us that Americans possess human qualities and are plain good people. I have more faith now that our countries can live together."

For something to remember me by, I gave Igor the stick with which I scored my first goal in Russian hockey. He was so excited. "Greatest gift," he kept saying. "Greatest gift."

I walked away convinced more than ever that Soviets are the same as you and I—people who want to be accepted, people who have the same feelings and needs we do. I allowed myself a further corny thought—if we had gotten to know each other as people, instead of letting suspicion and prejudice prevail, the cold war would have never happened. But you put a situation in the hands of scaremonger politicians on both sides and you get a half century of pointing nukes at one another.

I went to Leningrad to join up with Team U.S.A. I loved these guys, but I heard it all again, all the abuse about the Russians. "How could you have possibly lived here for a year?"

"This place sucks. Look at the people, they never smile."

"I'd rather be a bum in Florida than an average citizen in Leningrad. At least I could collect aluminum cans and take them in for a Zagnut at 7-Eleven."

"I know, I know, I know," I responded. "But you guys don't know the people."

When I got home to Minnesota, it was only four months before the second Russian revolution, four months before the people would be free.

Dimer, my old pal Khristich, called me from his hotel room where the Caps were staying. He had gotten over his ketchup-in-the-shoes trauma.

"Very happy," he said over and over. "I very happy in your country."

I wondered if he was going back to the Soviet Union for the summer. He laughed and said he had no such plans.

"And by the way," he asked. "How is my country?"

"Like you once told me, Dimer," I replied. "Country crazy. But people, big hearts."

INDEX